Dangerous Passage

Dangerous Passage

ISSUES IN THE ARCTIC

Gerard Kenney

NATURAL HERITAGE BOOKS

TORONTO

Published by Natural Heritage / Natural History Inc.
P.O. Box 95, Station O, Toronto, Ontario M4A 2M8
www.naturalheritagebooks.com

Library and Archives Canada Cataloguing in Publication

Kenney, Gerard I., 1931-
          Dangerous passage : issues in the Arctic / Gerard Kenney.

Includes bibliographical references and index.
ISBN 1-897045-13-1

          1. Northwest Passage. 2. Northwest Passage—Discovery and exploration. 3. Territory, National—Canada, Northern. 4. Environmental policy—Northwest Passage. I. Title.

FC3963.K448 2006   909'.096327   C2006-901176-1

Front cover: *Gjøa Sailing the Northwest Passage*, Lauritz Haaland, artist, 1906. *Courtesy of the Fram Museum, Oslo, Norway.*
Back cover: *The Louis St. Laurent*, Canada's largest icebreaker. *Courtesy of the Canadian Coast Guard.*
Cover and text design by Sari Naworynski
Edited by Jane Gibson
Printed and bound in Canada by Hignell Book Printing of Winnipeg

Natural Heritage / Natural History Inc. acknowledges the financial support of the Canada Council for the Arts and the Ontario Arts Council for our publishing program. We acknowledge the support of the Government of Ontario through the Ontario Media Development Corporation's Ontario Book Initiative. We also acknowledge the financial support of the Government of Canada through the Book Publishing Industry Development Program (BPIDP) and the Association for the Export of Canadian Books.

For Amanda, Jessica and young Cara – my three darling girls

Arctic Smoke & Mirrors (Prescott, ON: Voyageur Publishing, 1994)
Ships of Wood and Men of Iron (Toronto: Natural Heritage Books, 2005)

CONTENTS

LIST OF MAPS

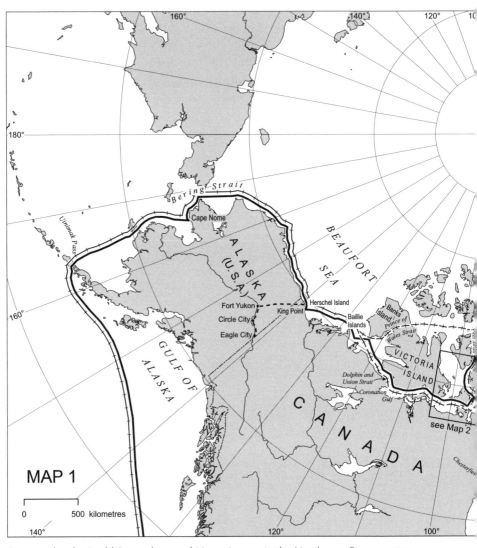

Routes taken by Roald Amundsen and Henry Larsen in the Northwest Passage. *Map by Tim West.*

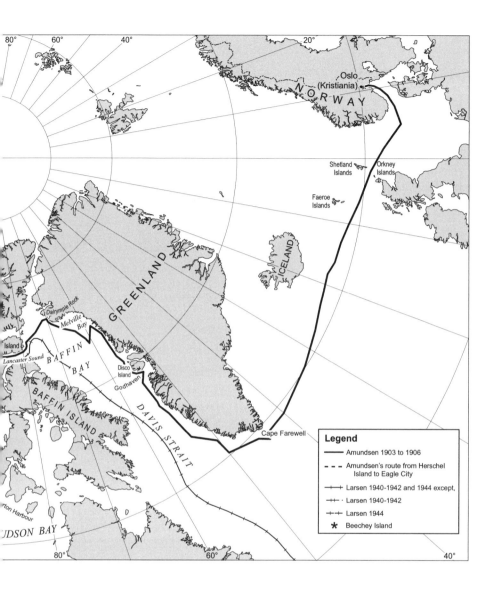

Detailed map of the area surrounding Gjoa Haven. *Map by Tim West.*

Foreword

In 2005, the Governor General of Canada, Her Excellency Adrienne Clarkson, on a trip to Nunavut had a cairn built at the edge of the Arctic Ocean. Fifty years ago, His Excellency, Vincent Massey, on his first trip as Governor General to the Canadian Arctic, had a canister dropped on the polar ice as a much less certain declaration – somewhat like the triangle at the top of Canadian maps of the day with their apex at the North Pole. Mr. Massey said his purpose was "to let the Americans know that Canada owns the High Arctic." It would not have had much weight in a legal context – much less than the voyages of the *Gjøa* and the *St. Roch*. However, the actions of governors general of our times are outward evidence of the continuing fact that Canada cannot be complacent about recognition of its sovereignty if global warming and dramatically shifting international oil prices alter the physical and economic circumstances of "our" Arctic.

There seems to be little doubt that the "circumstances" are indeed changing and that Canada will have to develop policies that will take into account all their many aspects and implications. Public knowledge and interest, neither of which exists at present, will be important for developing meaningful policies. *Dangerous Passage* is a significant contribution to both.

Gordon Robertson
Deputy Minister of Northern Affairs and National Resources,
and Commissioner of the Northwest Territories, 1953-1963.

Acknowledgements

Dr. George Hobson's much appreciated work of verifying the manuscript for this book was invaluable in ensuring its historical accuracy. For this I am very grateful. That said, I remain responsible for any inaccuracies that may have inadvertently been included in the final version.

Many thanks go to my friend and neighbour, Tim West, who spent many hours of his time creating excellent maps that allow the reader to follow the voyages of both Roald Amundsen and Henry Larsen as they sailed the dangerous passage.

Doreen Riedel was as helpful as usual with the part concerning her father, Henry Larsen, and his many adventures. Bernard Collin of the Canadian Coast Guard gets deserved thanks for finding and providing photographs of Arctic ships and a polar bear for Part III of the book. A thank you to Kåre Berg for permission to use two images from his book *Heroes of the Polar Wastes*, to the University of Toronto Press for permission to use a map from *Memoirs of a Very Civil Servant* by Gordon Robertson and to Fogarty's Cove Music for permission to use an excerpt from Stan Roger's "Northwest Passage."

My publisher/editors, Barry Penhale and Jane Gibson deserve a lot of credit for taking a bunch of words and some photos, and turning them into an attractive book, and for converting a business affair into a friendship in the process.

And finally the whole crew at Library and Archives Canada are much appreciated for their needed assistance in my research for textual and photographic items without which, the book could never have been written.

Introduction

One hundred years ago, in 1906, Norwegian Roald Amundsen emerged from the Arctic mists to announce to the world that he, and five crew members, in his tiny ship, *Gjøa,* had completed the first sea transit ever of the Northwest Passage, from ocean to ocean, Atlantic to Pacific.

Over the five hundred or so years that man searched for an elusive sea passage from Europe to Asia through the North American land mass, dozens of ships were lost and hundreds of mariners died in the search. The goal was understandable. It was an economic goal – to find a shorter, cheaper and more practical trading route between Europe and the Orient than those existing at the time. The two main routes at the time were: first, the extremely difficult and dangerous overland route, and later the extremely long and treacherous sea route around the Cape of Good Hope. Was there a better route?

Surely if the earth were round, one could sail from Europe to the Orient by going west rather than east. There was a major obstacle, though – the North American continent was squarely in the way. Imaginative dreamers got around that difficulty. In 1500, they imagined away any constraints by dreaming up a water route clear through the North American mainland leading to a short sea voyage to the Orient at the western end. They even gave this mythical passage a name – the Strait of Anian. It was just a matter of finding it.

The myth of Anian persisted until the latter part of the eighteenth century when Samuel Hearne walked 2,900 kilometres (1,800 miles) northwest from Hudson Bay to the mouth of the Coppermine River on the Arctic Ocean without crossing any such body of water. Hearne's findings laid Anian in its grave, but they still did not kill the desire to find a shorter sea route between Europe and the Orient. The search merely shifted to the waters of the Arctic Archipelago north of the

Canadian mainland. Finding such a sea route took on an aura of national pride and glory as Great Britain sent a large number of expeditions into the Arctic in the 1800s to look for the Northwest Passage, as the Brits dubbed it.

Over time, a sea passage stretching through the waters of the Archipelago and along the Canadian mainland's Arctic coast was eventually pieced together through the efforts of several explorers. But one crucial question remained unanswered until the early part of the twentieth century – could ships navigate this Northwest Passage to the extent that it could be used as an international shipping route between Europe and Asia? Two seagoing captains and their ships answered that question in the first half of the last century – a Norwegian, Roald Amundsen in the *Gjøa* and a Canadian of Norwegian birth, Henry Asbjorn Larsen, in the *St. Roch*. This book recounts the successful efforts of these two remarkable men to penetrate the Northwest Passage by ship from end to end, Amundsen in the east-west direction and Larsen in both directions, in the dying decades of an era when there were still ships of wood, and men of iron to sail them.

Now, in the twenty-first century, there is a renewed interest in the Northwest Passage as scientists throughout the world realize the rapidity with which global warming is affecting planet Earth and especially its polar regions. There are many unsettling issues facing the countries of the world, and especially Canada, concerning the future of the Northwest Passage in this time of melting ice caps, glaciers and sea ice in the Arctic. Canada in particular has a high stake in the foreseeable opening of the Passage to commercial navigation. There are estimates ranging from less than twenty years, and up, as to when the ice in the Passage will be thin enough to permit maritime traffic on an economic basis. The ice does not have to disappear completely to allow transiting ship traffic. It only has to get thin enough for icebreakers to be able to handle it effectively, and that will happen long before the ice disappears completely. In fact, technologically speaking, it is possible today for specially constructed ships to sail the Northwest Passage, but it is not yet economically feasible.

The latter part of this book addresses crucial issues that the

Canadian government must face in the very near future to ensure that our country has a strong and effective voice in controlling what happens in the Passage once ships, especially oil tankers, start using it. It is the shores of Canada that are on either side of the Passage. It is Canadian citizens who live, hunt and fish for sustenance along the Passage. An oil spill could be disastrous. Clearly, the Canadian government must move quickly on the many issues involved in an opening Passage. The United States, in fact, has a head start on Canada. It was in 1969 that we Canadians were brought down to earth with a shock when the Americans experimented with sending a huge oil tanker through the passage – the *Manhattan*. The experiment showed that it was not yet commercially practical to send large ships through the Passage at the time. But, as Bob Dylan has reminded us, "The times they are a-changin.' " It is certain the Americans have not forgotten about the Passage in the intervening years. The U.S. has undoubtedly been quietly doing its homework. Canada must take steps immediately to ensure that she is not caught unawares on this subject. It is already quite late in the game.

PART ONE

Roald Amundsen and the Gjøa, 1903–06

And now there came both mist and snow,
And it grew wondrous cold:
And ice, mast-high, came floating by,
As green as emerald.

– Samuel Taylor Coleridge, "The Rime of the Ancient Mariner"

CHAPTER ONE

The Silk Road
and the Strait of Anian

TRAVELLERS BY LAND FROM CHINA, THROUGH western Asia, and on to Europe always were, and still are today, confronted by a huge, hostile obstacle – the Taklimakan Desert. Sources of drinking water are buried deep in the desert, and they are few and far between in this arid hell. It is so hostile that few people have ever crossed that area in the memory of man. To get from the east side of the Taklimakan to the west, it is advisable to take the long route, bearing either north or south around the desert's edges, never straight across. Temperatures in the Taklimakan at times rise to oven-like 50° C (120° F), and at other times, plunge to depths of minus 20° or 25° C (minus 5° or 10° F). Taklimakan is said to mean "go in and you won't come out." A traveller to the desert once had this to report: "The continuous line of bones and bodies acted as a gruesome guide whenever we were uncertain of the route."[1] Even the mountain paths that skirt that impossible part of the world are not much easier. Steep, rocky, frozen mountain passes that would challenge mountain goats, let alone humans bypass the deadly hot sands.

The Silk Road has been a trading route for the flow of goods between China, western Asia and Europe for two millennia or more, and one still has to contend with the Taklimakan or the frozen mountain passes. Few were the traders who ever travelled the entire route from the Far East to Europe, or vice-versa. Individual traders moved goods only part of the way, east or west, before exchanging them with a neighbouring group of traders who then turned around and moved the goods another step closer to their destination, like links in a chain. After many such exchanges, and the passage of months, if not years, small quantities of these goods eventually trickled into the markets of Eastern China, or conversely, of western Asia and Europe. Western peoples, particularly the Romans, were seduced by the exotic eastern merchandise that they did not normally find in their local markets, such as silk, the texture of which they found so beautiful, fine and soft to the skin. One can surmise that silk from the east must have been a major item of trade carried over this route for it to be baptized the Silk Road, but it was far from being the only item. The Chinese were equally seduced by western marvels such as ivory, gold, gems, furs and glass, the latter being unknown in China at the time. In return, the Orientals sent teas, spices, jade, porcelain, lacquer, bronze, gunpowder and other exotic treasures in addition to silk, in the opposite direction. More than goods traversed along the Silk Road. People, cultures, art, religions, philosophies and ideas were exchanged across the borders of seventeen countries stretching some 11,300 kilometres (7,000 miles). This oldest of commercial land arteries was the main highway along which Buddhism spread from northwestern India through all of central Asia and into China. The religious philosophies of Islam, Christianity, Zoroastrianism and Confucianism also made their way West by means of the Silk Road.

In the thirteenth century, Marco Polo and his family undertook a remarkable odyssey from Italy through western Asia and on, all the way to the court of Kublai Khan at Cambaluc near Peking (now Beijing). Seventeen years later, the Polos were allowed to leave China and Marco went back by a southern water route through the Indian Ocean, along the coast of India and north to Europe. This had hardly been a mere trading journey – he returned home 24 years after leaving Italy, long after having been given up for dead. He was minus his oriental trade goods when he arrived home. Bandits along the way had stolen them from him, but he had fantastic tales to tell.

The transfer of goods around and through the inhospitable wastes of Asia, and on to Europe, was painfully slow, uncertain, expensive and subject to banditry as Marco Polo found out. With obstacles such as these, it is no wonder that Europeans dreamed of other ways to reach the Orient. European trade with eastern Asia became somewhat more practical, although it was still a very long and dangerous trip, after Vasco da Gama discovered the sea route around the southern extremity of Africa in the sixteenth century. Over the years, as the concept of a round Earth became more accepted in the old world, the possibilities for more efficient trade offered by this geometric feature was not lost on more advanced thinkers, and in particular, mariners. Land found by sailing south, then east, around the Cape of Good Hope, and north could theoretically also be found using a shorter, quicker, more direct western water route. And indeed it could – theoretically.

What Columbus did not know in 1492, of course, was how far he would have to travel if he went west to reach the marvellous treasures of the East, and how many obstacles would block his path. It's just as well he was unaware of these or he might never have set out. The estimate in his day was that it was some 6,000 kilometres (3,600 miles) from Europe to India going west. No wonder he thought he had arrived when he reached the West Indies.

Although Columbus never reached the Orient, many after him – Frobisher, Hudson, Cartier, the Cabots – John and Sebastian – and a host of others from a number of European countries all set out with that same goal in mind, only instead of sailing southwest as Columbus did, they tended north of west and found New France, Baffin Island and Hudson Bay. The inland sea of Hudson Bay looked particularly promising. It headed in the right direction and quite possibly could give rise to a passage on its western shore that opened up on a small sea across which beckoned the far east, almost within sight. In the sixteenth century, a myth arose that imagined such a passage of open water cutting east-west across the newly discovered North American land mass from Hudson Bay to a western sea facing an Asiatic shore, that was, it was hoped, not too far west.

Cartographers of the time even showed such a waterway on their maps which Spanish navigators dubbed the "Strait of Anian." Martin Frobisher, Henry Hudson, Jacques Cartier, John and Sebastian Cabot, Luke Foxe, Thomas James, James Knight and others were all looking for this strait when they left European shores and sailed west, only to be frustrated in their quests since the Strait of Anian just didn't exist. But nobody knew this, until Samuel Hearne returned from his land voyage to the Arctic Ocean in 1772. Hearne had walked and paddled a round trip of 5,800 kilometres (3,600 miles) from Fort Prince of Wales on the west coast of Hudson Bay to the shores of the Arctic Ocean, and back again, without running into the mythical strait. Thus was disproved the myth of the Strait of Anian. There was no open water route cutting through the solid rock of the North American continent.

From that time on, the search for an open sea passage between the Atlantic and Pacific moved farther north into the waters of the Arctic Ocean and among the channels separating the Arctic Islands. Perhaps a Strait of Anian could be found there, or as the British called it, a Northwest Passage. By the mid-1800s, every stretch of the Arctic coast of the Canadian mainland had been explored in bits and pieces by a host of explorers – with one exception. There was a gap of some 100 kilometres (60 miles) where it was uncertain whether or not there was an open water passage between the coast and King William Island. It was thought that a barrier of land closed off this stretch. That question was finally settled by John Rae[2] in the spring of 1854 during an overland expedition from the south – yes, there was indeed a water route stretching the whole length of Canada's Arctic coastline and through the waters of the Archipelago. The previously undiscovered gap became known as Rae Strait, which was the final link in a chain of piecemeal discoveries of the Northwest Passage. But that answer alone would not have satisfied the mariners of old who searched so assiduously, and with such tragic loss of lives, for a water route that would allow ships to carry on commercial trade between Europe and the

Orient. The more important and practical question would have been "was it possible for large ships of trading goods to navigate the Northwest Passage?" as it came to be known. That was a question the Norwegian, Roald Amundsen, set out to answer when he and his crew eased his ship the *Gjøa* out of Oslo harbour one June night in 1903. His goal was to become the first to successfully sail a ship the whole length of the Northwest Passage from the Atlantic Ocean to the Pacific.

Many had tried to find and sail the Northwest Passage – William Parry, John Ross, John Franklin, Robert McClure and others – and all failed, spectacularly in the case of Franklin. It was left to Amundsen and his crew of six – with little Arctic experience among them other than what they had read in books – to crack the secret of sailing the Northwest Passage during a three-year voyage from 1903 to 1906, aboard the tiny 47-ton sloop *Gjøa*.

CHAPTER TWO

Preparing for the Great Adventure

ROALD AMUNDSEN WAS BORN IN 1872 AT BORGE, near the town of Sarpsborg in southeast Norway. From a young age, Arctic regions fascinated him. At the age of fifteen, Amundsen discovered the works of John Franklin and was thrilled by them. Franklin's words were destined to mould the rest of Amundsen's life. From age fifteen on, Arctic exploration and being an Arctic explorer, became Amundsen's overriding passions. He did not let his mother in on his secret desire – his father was no longer living – because he knew she would not share his enthusiasm about the north. His mother's dream for her son was that he become a doctor. Despite his mother's wishes, the future explorer started his northern preparations while still living at home. Norway, like Canada, is a cold country, where homes were, and still are, kept completely tight against the cold of winter, but Amundsen slept with his window wide open to harden his body to its future environment.

The budding explorer entered medical school to please his mother, but when she died two years later, he lost no time in shifting gears. He felt that he was now released to follow his own true calling, but he soon found his path detoured for a time while he put in his compulsory military training. Even this he turned to advantage in preparing for his future; as he put it, "because I wanted to be a good citizen and because I felt that military training would be of great benefit to me as further preparation for life."[3]

During a Christmas break, he and a friend foolishly plunged into a poorly planned local adventure as a preparatory exercise for Arctic exploration, an adventure that nearly put an early end to his Arctic career before it even started. A few hundred kilometres from Oslo slept a wild and barren plateau, some 2,000 metres (6,500 feet) high and 120 kilometres (75 miles) wide, where there lived not a soul in the late 1800s except for a few Lapp herdsmen, or Saami as they are known today, who grazed their reindeer there during the summer. The plateau is named Hardangervidda. The only building on the plateau at the time was a lonely, rudimentary hut in the middle of it where these herdsmen lived while their reindeer fattened up on the vegetation. But in the frigid months of winter, there was no one in the interior of the plateau. On the eastern edge, at the base, there lived a peasant farmer, his wife and their two married sons, a total of six people. On the western extremity there was another peasant farm near the top of the plateau. Amundsen's plan was to travel from Oslo to the farm at the foot of the east side to spend a night, and leave the following morning to climb the steep slope up to the plateau itself, ski to the hut in the middle and bivouac for the night with his friend. Then, on the second day, they would ski on across the rest of the plateau to the farm on the west. The plan seemed simple and straightforward, but the pair botched its execution, helped in that by almost malignant weather.

Right from the beginning things did not go well. Waking up in the morning at the farm on the east, and all set to go, they were greeted by a raging blizzard that had swept in overnight. On the top of the plateau the storm was no doubt more like an icy hurricane. They delayed their departure. Gale winds and snow raged on for the next eight days. On the ninth day, the storm abated and, despite the combined voices of experience of the three men of the house warning them of the deadly dangers on the plateau at that time of the year, the adventurous pair forsook the security of the farmhouse, climbed up onto the flat plain without too much trouble and set a compass course for the herders' hut in the centre of it. They thought their task quite simple and counted on at most two days to reach the farmhouse on the western edge of the plateau with an overnight stop at the herders' hut halfway across. They had provisioned themselves accordingly with equipment and food, which meant they had precious little of either. A sleeping bag each and an alcohol lamp, but no tent, was the sum total of their equipment. Their food supply was just as elaborate – a few crackers, some chocolate bars and a bit of butter.

With map and compass in hand and friendly weather, they were able to find the hut without problem, reaching it in the early evening. Getting in, however, was another matter. Heavy boards were nailed securely over the door, window and even chimney openings. Without tools, it was not easy work to clear away these obstructions, but, with a lot of exertion and time, they succeeded. Fortunately for them, a supply of firewood had been stacked in the hut and eventually a roaring fire was going, but the achievement was not without difficulty. It is not always the easiest thing to start a fire under a cold chimney when the mercury is heading for the depths of the thermometer – it was −23° C (−8° F) with an icy wind blasting down the flue. Considering their food list, they could not have had a very revitalizing supper to cheer them up. With bones and muscles aching from exertion, bodies stretched out before a warm and flickering fire, the budding explorers easily slipped off into a deep sleep.

The morning did not bode well. The blizzard had returned and they could not move from their temporary sanctuary. It was obvious that food was going to be a problem. Rummaging around in the various nooks and crannies of the hut, they had the good fortune to find a small bag of flour, which became the source of their meals for the next few days in the unappetizing form of a watery gruel. On the third day, the weather had improved enough for the adventurers to push forward, using map and compass to head for the featureless spot on the western edge of the plateau where the farm was located. It had been built at one of the only two places on the plateau where it was possible to scramble down from the western edge to the valley below.

The temperature soon rose and snow started falling, which proved fatal for their flimsy paper map that they had to consult regularly to find their way. It was soon a useless, soggy handful of pulp. This was a serious blow to their ability to navigate with any accuracy, but they skied on. The pair did not reach the farm on the western edge of the plateau that day, so when evening darkness closed in on them, they had to unroll their sleeping bags and flop them down right on the snow out in the open and spend their time there without shelter. It was a right miserable night they had, wet to the bones in their sleeping bags, bellies grumbling for food. Somehow they managed to lose their bags of what little food they had under the snow – never to be found again. Gone was the small comfort that chewing on a few scraps of food would have brought.

Things were becoming life-threatening and they began to fear death from starvation and freezing. The next day the adventurers stubbornly headed west trying to reach the farm on the western edge of the plateau. With snow beginning to fall heavily and lacking basic navigation equipment since their map had disintegrated, they finally decided to turn around and retrace their steps back to the eastern farm from which they had set out five days before.

They trudged only a few exhausting kilometres before falling darkness forced them again to camp in the open for the night, this time in the lee of a small hummock to break the howling wind. Amundsen tried to improve on his situation by scooping out a small cave in the snow just big enough to fit his body and sleeping bag. At least he was completely out of the wind. Relatively sheltered and warm, the tired trekker fell into a deep sleep on a desperately cold night with falling temperatures. When he awoke in the morning, he panicked at finding himself solidly frozen into what could easily turn into a coffin of ice. He couldn't budge. He called out to his companion who couldn't find him at first. To Amundsen's great good fortune, his companion had not made the same mistake. He had slept a bit less comfortably perhaps, but he did not wake up a prisoner of ice. After tracing the muffled cries, he started digging and after a couple of hours of frantic scraping with his hands, finally freed his imprisoned partner.

The by now sorry looking pair trudged on in the morning and by nightfall had fortunately come upon a small shanty (actually it was part of the farm they had originally visited although they did not know it at the time) with ski tracks around it. Here they were able survive the night in comparative safety, although very hungry. The following morning, Amundsen left his weakening partner in the shanty and followed the ski tracks until they eventually led him to one of the men from the eastern farm, from which they had started out seven days before. Amundsen hurried back to get his flagging friend and together they returned to his saviour on skis who took them back to the little farm. The two haggard creatures were unrecognizable. The other members of the family had to be told who they were.

It had been a hard way to prepare for Arctic service, but the lessons learned were most certainly not lost on Amundsen, the future polar explorer. His next stint of preparation for polar service, in the Antarctic this time, would again prove to be a misadventure, building up his experience of how not to do things – experiences that were not without value.

Amundsen read voraciously about polar exploration and came to the conclusion that it was a mistake for commanders of Arctic expeditions to not also be ship's captains. A simple way of looking at the difference between the two functions is that the commander decides where to go, while the captain decides how and when to get there. The captain could refuse to carry out the commander's orders if he believed they could compromise the safety of the ship. Many expeditions sailed with both a commander and a captain of the ship, two different persons in decision-making roles. This very often led to a division of responsibility with diverging opinions and attendant friction between the two leaders and the factions of their respective supporters among the officers and crew. To avoid making what he considered to be a serious mistake, Amundsen decided that he would have to become a ship's captain himself before undertaking the leadership of an Arctic expedition. To do that, he decided that he had to start by first gaining significant experience before the mast.

For three summers, from 1894 to 1896, Amundsen signed on as a simple sailor aboard the old *Magdalena,* which went sealing in Arctic waters, and he worked his way up to a rating of first mate. In 1897 at the age of 25, he found himself a berth as first mate aboard the *Belgica* of the Belgian Antarctic Expedition that was setting out to explore the south magnetic pole. The ship's doctor was Frederick Cook who was later to attain international polar fame – some would say, infamy – when he declared he had discovered the North Pole the year before Peary claimed that it was he who was the discoverer. The ship was a veritable "Tower of Babel" with six languages spoken aboard – English, French, Polish, Romanian, Norwegian and Flemish. It is a wonder orders could be carried out at all.

The shortest way from Belgium to the South Magnetic Pole in the South Pacific Ocean, south of Australia, was through the Mediterranean Sea, the Suez Canal and southeast across the Indian Ocean to the pole. The commander of the expedition, a Belgian named Adrien de Gerlache de Gomery, who was not the ship's captain, had his own agenda besides the main one of the finding the South Magnetic Pole. He decided to go the long way around instead via Cape Horn on the southern tip of South America, stopping in Tierra del Fuego for six weeks during the southern summer. He wanted to add to the world's knowledge of this relatively unknown land by collecting botanical and biological specimens, mapping the area and taking meteorological readings. These unplanned delays were going to have a decidedly negative effect on the expedition as the southern winter crept up on them.

Finally continuing south, the expedition mapped a part of the coast of Antarctica before sailing west toward its destination south of Australia. By this time the winter season was hard upon them and icebergs populated the sea. One night, with an inexperienced seaman at the helm while the rest of the crew slept, the ship managed to slip over a ledge of ice between two icebergs and end up becalmed and trapped in a basin between the two mountains of ice. As Amundsen put it, "by very careful maneuvring, we succeeded in extricating ourselves, but only to fall into a more serious situation."

As the *Belgica* skirted the edge of the southern ice field, a terrific

The photograph of Roald Amundsen that was used as the frontispiece of his book, *The North West Passage.*

gale blew up. The wise thing would have been to sail the ship north away from the crushing dangers of the ice field, but both the commander and the captain agreed to try another tactic instead and sailed the ship south into an opening in the ice field to get away from the gale-fed waves. This move, prompted by rank inexperience in polar sailing, moved them away from the waves all right, but it also got them stuck deep in the ice field where the expedition was destined to spend the next 13 months – a predicament for which they were not prepared. Passing the winter in Antarctica was not part of the plan. The men were not provisioned with winter clothes nor was there enough food to last such a long time at sea. Two sailors lost their minds and the whole crew suffered from scurvy.

Both Amundsen and Cook knew from reading that the threat of scurvy could be kept at bay by eating fresh meat rare, cooked as little as possible. Many of the abundant seals and penguins were killed and brought back to the ship, but the commander had a great aversion to eating meat and forbade it for the entire crew. The scurvy became so bad that both the commander and the ship's captain took to their beds and wrote their wills. With the two leaders out of commission, the command of the expedition fell upon Amundsen's shoulders as ranking officer.

It was under these desperate conditions that Amundsen and Dr. Cook got to know and appreciate each other. They both thought the same way and Cook was particularly resourceful. Amundsen made up a work crew of the few who were still strong enough to work and had them dig through the snow to disinter the carcasses of penguins and seals and bring them aboard for food. Everyone on the ship including the commander was immediately fed this meat and within a week the health of all was on the upswing. Amundsen developed an affection and respect for Cook that was never shaken even in later years when Cook was reviled for supposedly faking his discovery of the North Pole. As Amundsen put it:

> It was in this fearful emergency, during these thirteen long months in which almost the certainty of death stared us steadily in the face, that I came to know Dr. Cook intimately and to form the affection for him and the gratitude to him, which nothing in his later career could ever cause me to alter. He, of all the ship's company, was the one man of unfaltering courage, unfailing hope, endless cheerfulness, and unwearied kindness. When anyone was sick, he was at his bedside to comfort him; when any was disheartened, he was there to encourage and inspire. And not only was his faith undaunted, but his ingenuity and enterprise were boundless. With the return of the sun after the long Antarctic night, he led small parties on scouting expeditions in all directions looking for evidences that the ice might providentially open and leave a channel for us back to the open sea.[4]

When a small basin of open water formed some 900 metres from the ship, it was Cook who foresaw that a crack from the open sea in the spring-weakened, surrounding ice would probably lead to that basin. To be in a position to take advantage of this occurrence, he proposed that a channel be cut through the ice leading to the open water and that the *Belgica* be towed to the basin, ready to sail down the crack to the ocean when the time came.

Although the rest of the crew, including Amundsen, were not convinced and did not yet have confidence in Dr. Cook at this stage, they all turned out anyway to cut the channel. They made quite a sight dressed as they were in bright red suits. Since there were no winter clothes on board, Amundsen had had a supply of scarlet woollen blankets cut up and sewn into loose suits for the men. It was a strange uniform they wore, but they were warm. It took several weeks to create the channel with large hand saws and sticks of dynamite. When the job was done, the men strained and pulled the *Belgica* with ropes to her new home in the basin. More long weeks passed without change in the ice conditions, but then one day exactly what Cook had foreseen came to pass – the ice cracked all the way from the open sea right to *Belgica's* basin. The crew lost no time in sailing down the lead to the sea. They were finally free to go and ecstatically sailed for Europe arriving back home in 1899, two years after their departure.

Had Amundsen and Cook not been on board, there is scarcely a doubt but that the *Belgica* would have gone down in history as another of those enigmatic cases of disappearing expeditions. Again Amundsen had gained invaluable experience in preparation for the Arctic – the hard way.

The year following his return, he got his sea skipper's licence. Methodically, step by step, and with impeccable logic, Amundsen was building a solid foundation for his first Arctic expedition. Next, he enlisted the support of Norway's "Grand Old Man of Arctic exploration," Fridtjof Nansen,[5] who, because of his national reputation as an explorer *sans pareil,* would be invaluable to the success of fundraising efforts that would be necessary to finance Amundsen's voyage.

Amundsen realized that to attract funds to his venture, it would have to be more than just a voyage of exploration to sail the Northwest Passage; it had to have a solid scientific purpose. The budding explorer decided that his scientific objective would be "to make the conclusive observations of the true location of the North Magnetic Pole." With this purpose, Amundsen went to Hamburg, Germany, and convinced the director of the Deutsche Seewarte Institute,[6] the renowned Geheimrath George von Neumayer, to admit him to his prestigious academy to study magnetic science and learn the methods of taking magnetic observations. For three months under the wing of von Neumayer, Amundsen honed his skills.

He then bought the scientific instruments he would need for his magnetic observations. His next job was to find a suitable vessel for his purposes, which he did in 1900. She was a small fishing boat displacing 47 tons and the same age as he, 28 years, and was named the *Gjøa*. She was a single-masted sloop that had spent a good part of her life as a herring boat. Shortly after he bought her, Amundsen took his ship on a summer trip into polar waters and found that he was fully satisfied with her performance.

During the preparatory phase for his great adventure, Amundsen fell into periods of despair – funds were not coming in to keep step with expenses. He had borrowed heavily to buy supplies for the trip and now his creditors started applying pressure on him to be paid. The most important of his creditors threatened to throw a lien on the *Gjøa* and have Amundsen arrested for fraud if he was not paid within 24 hours. This situation had the potential to destroy his many years of hard work and cause him to cancel the expedition. Amundsen went over the situation in his mind – hounds were at the door, the *Gjøa* was already provisioned with food and equipment for five years, the dog pemmican was already on board, as were the sled dogs; everything was ready to go, albeit not fully paid for. Amundsen reacted in the only way possible if his plans were not to be thwarted. At midnight on June 16, 1903, the *Gjøa* and her crew quietly slipped her moorings under the cover of the darkness and secretly stood out of Kristiania Harbour (sometimes spelled Christiania, today called Oslo) – and headed for the high seas.

> The ruin of my many years of work seemed imminent. I grew desperate and I resolved upon a desperate expedient. I summoned my six carefully chosen companions, explained my predicament, and asked if they would co-operate with me in my strategy. They enthusiastically

agreed. Therefore, at midnight on June 16th, in the midst of a perfect deluge of rain, we seven conspirators made our way to the wharf where the *Gjøa* was tied, went aboard, cast off the hawsers, and turned southward toward Skagger Rack and the North Sea. When dawn arose on our truculent creditor, we were safely out on the open main, seven as lighthearted pirates as ever flew the black flag, disappearing upon a quest that should take us three years and on which we were destined to succeed in an enterprise that has baffled our predecessors for four centuries.

CHAPTER THREE

Underway at Last!

AMUNDSEN'S CREW OF SIX INCLUDED FIVE Norwegians and one Dane:

- First Lieutenant Godfred Hansen, 27, the Dane, second in command of the expedition, was skilled in navigation, astronomy, geology and photography;
- Anton Lund, 39, who had many years of experience as skipper and harpoonist in the Arctic Ocean;
- Peter Ristvedt, 30, the expedition's meteorologist and first engineer;
- Helmer Hansen, second mate, with many years of sailing in the Arctic Ocean;
- Gustav Juel Wiik, 24, second engineer and Amundsen's assistant for magnetic observations;
- Adolf Henrik Lindstrøm, 38, cook, who had just returned the year before on Otto Sverdrup's second Arctic expedition where he had served in the galley on board the *Fram*.

Roald Amundsen and his
crew ready to get underway.
From left to right, front row:
Godfred Hansen, Roald
Amundsen; back row:
Peder Ristvedt, Adolf
Henrik Lindstrøm, Anton
Lund, Helmer Hansen
and Gustav Juel Wiik.
From Heroes of the Polar
Wastes *by Kåre Berg.*

Amundsen himself was 31 years old.

The high-spirited seven had escaped to the freedom of the open sea where no one could stop them and they well knew it. After leaving Norwegian waters, Amundsen and his crew headed due west toward the southern tip of Greenland, Cape Farewell. Their new-found freedom from the constraints of civilization and bureaucracy rested lightly on their shoulders and hearts as they headed for high adventure.

The North Sea provided the requisite gales in that part of the ocean and the *Gjøa* rolled like a drunken sailor, soon separating the true seamen from the landlubbers. Once the ship was underway, the six dogs on board were set free. They roamed the deck and took a lively interest in the men, especially the landlubbers. The canines' meals of cod and water did not much appease their hunger, and seasickness among members of the crew provided the occasional, and much appreciated, extra meal for the dogs.

Amundsen was a believer in freedom of action as his nighttime departure suggests and he did not drive his men by the rule of law. He knew, as many leaders of expeditions did not, that a regime of strict discipline is not the way to get the best out of good men.

> As a result of my own experience I had determined to
> apply the system of freedom on board as far as possible,
> to let everyone feel that he was independent in his own
> sphere. This creates among sensible people a voluntary

spirit of discipline of far greater value than enforced rule. Everyone thus obtains the consciousness that he is a man who is depended upon as a thinking being and not as a wound-up machine. The zeal for work is doubled and so is the work itself.

On June 25 the expedition passed into the real Atlantic as it left the Orkneys astern. The wind was fair and the *Gjøa* relied mostly on her sails with occasional assistance from the ship's 13 hp internal combustion engine when the wind weakened. The power of maritime engines of those days seems so low when compared to the horsepower ratings of today's automobiles, but they served their purpose. On July 11, Greenland's Cape Farewell was sighted. That part of the Atlantic is always well supplied with floes of drift ice that float down from the east coast of Greenland. Many of these floes can be shouldered aside by a ship designed for Arctic service as the *Gjøa* was, but care must be taken to avoid the bigger chunks that could seriously damage so small a ship.

This ever-present ice field south of Cape Farewell seems to affect Norwegian sailors in a strange way. In 1898, Otto Sverdrup had reported that he could see a multitude of shapes in the ice floes as they drifted past his ship, the *Fram*, including "a church and spire, a sleeping princess in snow white garb, an Akvavit bottle on a platter, a bullock's carcass with four legs in the air, tables, sofa, chairs, a horse mushroom, herds of polar bears and wolves"[7] – an endless procession. Some 35 years later, a Canadian of Norwegian birth, Henry Larsen, who sailed the *St. Roch* through the Northwest Passage in both directions, would write that he saw, "towering cathedrals with magnificent spires, battleships, bears or dancing girls."[8] Amundsen's trip did not depart from the norm in this respect. On July 24 a cry went up, "A sail ahead!" This was followed by, "A full-rigged ship!" And then, "I see clearly, it is a brig." A few minutes later, "There's another!" All the telescopes aboard the *Gjøa* were quickly pressed into service. After a few moments of silent scrutiny, one of the telescopes was heard snapping shut in a decisive manner. "Gentlemen," announced Lieutenant Hansen, "it is an iceberg!"

Visitors from Greenland on board the
Gjøa. From The North West Passage *by Roald
Amundsen.*

The following day, July 25, the *Gjøa* entered Godhavn Harbour,
Greenland, situated on a small island across a narrow strait from the
much larger Disco Island. Godhavn, a town of 108 people in 1903, was
the home of the inspector of North Greenland as well as the governor
of the colony. The previous year, Amundsen had been in contact with
the inspector and had arranged for ten dogs complete with harnesses
and sleds, some kayaks, skis and twenty barrels of fuel to be assembled
in Godhavn for the expedition. For the next six days, Amundsen and
his crew were busy getting their new dogs, equipment and fuel on
board where they were stored in ship-shape fashion. The water tanks
were topped up. Magnetic and astronomical observations were taken.
It was not all work, though. Time was taken to visit, socialize and
barter with the inhabitants both whites and Inuit, with Norwegian and
Inuktitut words flying back and forth with no regard for the language
barrier. Despite this, much successful trading took place. Amundsen
described their stay in Godhavn as "altogether a pleasant one."

The Greenlanders did not take such rare visits lightly. As the *Gjøa*
stood out to sea from Godhavn Harbour to continue on her northern
voyage, the Norwegians saw that the public buildings had been deco-
rated with bunting for the occasion and they heard the thunder of an
official salute of *adieu* fired off by the Greenlanders in their honour.

Amundsen had one more place to visit on the coast of Greenland before crossing Baffin Bay over to Canada to enter the Northwest Passage, and that was Dalrymple Rock. To get there, though, involved crossing one of the most dangerous stretches of Arctic water. No sailor of the time ever entered lightly upon a crossing of Melville Bay. There were always attendant risks. Leonard Gutteridge writes in *Ghosts of Cape Sabine*: "That large and ever turbulent stretch of water 300 miles wide was considered a graveyard of lost ships, 'a mysterious reign of terror' Elisha Kane had called it. In the English explorer Clements Markham's words, 'Many a well-equipped ship has been caught in its fatal embrace. What tales of woe and disaster could its icy waters unfold.' In one year alone nineteen vessels were lost in Melville Bay, some crushed between massive icebergs, others hammered into the depths by frigid winds."[9]

Melville Bay was entered with trepidation on August 8. It wasn't long before the *Gjøa* was dodging ice and looking for open leads to sail in, at times with pea-soup fog coming in to add its dramatic dimension to the mix. The crossing was not an easy one, though relatively an innocuous one according to Melville Bay standards. By four o'clock in the afternoon on August 15, the bay's 490 dangerous kilometres (300 miles) of width had been conquered. Contrary to its reputation, the bay was quite benign that August in 1903 and Dalrymple Rock was soon reached. Amundsen was clearly relieved:

> We had every reason to be pleased; that portion of the sea had always appeared to me as the most difficult to get through, with such a small ship as ours, in the whole North West Passage. And now we had navigated it without mishap.

Unimpressive Dalrymple Rock off the coast of Greenland was a traditional rendezvous of the Scottish whaling fleet. Its importance to Amundsen was that before he departed Oslo, he had arranged with two Scottish whalers to leave him fuel and equipment there to top up what *Gjøa* and her crew would have used in crossing the Atlantic. He wanted his tiny ship to be loaded to the gunwales with supplies before pointing her prow into the Northwest Passage for God-only-knew how many months without the capability of provisioning herself with even one match, let alone anything else – the one exception being meat. This the North could provide and the Norwegians planned to hunt for it.

As the *Gjøa* approached Dalrymple Rock, the lookout in the crow's nest cried out, "Two kayaks ahead!" The whole crew stampeded onto the deck and welcomed the Inuit paddlers aboard. Amundsen thought them "two really good-looking men." A moment of high comedy occurred when an Inuk bent over to pick up a knife he had dropped and inadvertently mooned the crew of the *Gjøa* due to the worn-out condition of his pants. The two men seemed very excited and in a gush of incomprehensible Inuktitut, tried to tell the crew something that was obviously of importance. Finally, one of the Inuit cracked a wide smile and uttered one word – "Mylius." This made perfect sense to Amundsen and his crew, and overjoyed them. It was not unexpected that the Danish so-called Literacy Expedition to Greenland under Mylius Erichsen[10] would be in the neighbourhood.

> Scarcely had the name been uttered, when there burst forth a rattle of fire-arms, as if a regular battle were raging behind a piled mass of ice, and six kayaks issued from among it like flashes of lightening. One of the kayaks was decked with a little Norse flag, and another with the Danish flag. It was in truth a pleasant surprise. We soon had on board the leader of the expedition Mylius Erichsen, and one of its members, Knut [sic] Rasmussen, together with four Eskimo.

Knud Rasmussen was a half-Inuit Greenlander who was on his first Arctic expedition that was to last from 1902 to 1904. Later in 1910, he and storyteller/trader Peter Freuchen[11] would establish a trading post at Thule from which Rasmussen would travel far and wide studying the culture and language of various Inuit groups. He was to become famous as an ethnologist for the work he and a group of scientists did during the four-year Fifth Thule Expedition, which set out in 1921. The expedition ranged across the North from Greenland to Alaska. One of Rasmussen's major findings was that the Inuit from Greenland right through to the west coast all spoke essentially the same language, even though the speakers didn't know they did. The variations between the different dialects were enough to inhibit mutual comprehension at first, but with a short period of adjustment, people who spoke one dialect found that they could in fact converse with those of another dialect. Rasmussen was able to determine this because Inuktitut was his mother tongue and he spoke the Greenland dialect. Despite his native dialect, he was able to converse with people of all dialects right across the Arctic to Alaska.

Amundsen had a cache of supplies awaiting him on Dalrymple Rock. There were 105 cases of equipment and food to be on-loaded, each of which weighed on average 115 kilograms (250 pounds), with some tipping the scales at almost 180 kilograms (400 pounds), plus six barrels of fuel. His crew and the four visiting Inuit started working at ten o'clock in the evening and the following morning at eight o'clock they had almost finished. They had only eleven cases of supplies and the fuel left to load when a dangerous onshore wind started blowing. There were no chances to be taken. Amundsen and his crew quickly hoisted sail and barely escaped from the precarious position the *Gjøa* found herself in and sailed around to the lee side of the islet. The cases and barrels of fuel were now much farther away from the ship and had to be muscled quite some distance across the rocky islet to its new anchorage. What would have taken about an hour at their previous anchorage took them until seven o'clock that evening to finish. The *Gjøa* was now carrying 19,300 litres (4,246 gallons) of fuel, a dangerous cargo indeed as the crew was to realize some time later.

Amundsen's next task was to sail his ship west across the wind-furrowed expanse of Baffin Bay and reach the protection of Lancaster Sound on the Canadian side as quickly as possible. The ship had next to no freeboard and was in a poor position to do battle with a storm should one arise. At 2:30 in the morning of August 17, the *Gjøa* struck out across the openness of the bay and hoped for the best. The crossing took three days and by four o'clock on the morning of August 20, she entered the protection of Lancaster Sound, the beginning of the Northwest Passage, and set a course for Beechey Island on the southwestern coast of Devon Island.

Beechey is really an island only at high tide and becomes a peninsula of Devon Island when the tide is low. It holds a special place in Arctic history for having been the first port of call for many ships entering the Northwest Passage in search of Franklin's expedition. In 1845–46, Sir John Franklin's *Erebus* and *Terror* spent the first winter of their ill-fated voyage of discovery at Beechey. Three of his crew died that first winter and are buried there – John Torrington, John Hartnell and William Braine. Their corpses lay there in peace until 1984 when Canadian scientists carefully exhumed the body of John Torrington and found it to be almost perfectly preserved by the permafrost it had lain in for the previous 138 years. In 1986, the bodies of Hartnell and Braine were dug up and also found to be excellently preserved. Autopsies performed on the bodies showed that all three men died of a combination of tuberculosis, lead poisoning from tin cans that food came in, and finally pneumonia, which finished them off. There is a fourth grave on Beechey; sailor Thomas Morgan from Robert McClure's *Investigator* was buried there in 1854 after falling into the sea and drowning. This grave was not dug up because the scientists who worked on the other three wanted to examine only bodies from the Franklin expedition to determine the cause of death of its crew members. There is also a fifth mound of earth there that looks suspiciously like a grave, but nothing is known about what may lie under that additional raised mass of soil.

Because Beechey Island was visited by practically every ship entering the Arctic in search of Franklin, its exact longitude was accurately pinpointed early on, using precise time provided by the dozens of fresh chronometers on ships just arrived from England. Latitude was not a problem. Sailors had been able to determine accurate latitude for centuries by taking sun shots with sextants or other similar instruments, but figuring out longitude accurately depended on knowing accurate time from fresh chronometers.

In Otto Sverdrup's 1902 expedition, after having been in the Arctic for almost four years, the inaccuracies that had crept into the chronometers on board *Fram* over that period had rendered them useless for accurate navigating. While the ship was still locked in the ice of Goose Fiord on Ellesmere Island four years after departure from Norway, Sverdrup sent a team of men by dog team to Beechey Island to correct their chronometers. By using the precisely known longitude of Beechey, together with star charts, they were able to determine the precise time from stellar observations, and to correct their chronometers, thus restoring accuracy to their mapping and navigation.

Amundsen had no need to correct his chronometers since he was only about two months out of port and they were still accurate, but he probably checked them just the same. On August 22, at nine o'clock in the evening the *Gjøa* dropped anchor in Erebus and Terror Bay of Beechey Island, named after Franklin's ships. Though his crew turned in for a much deserved and undisturbed night of sleep, Amundsen stayed awake for a while, peering ashore, awed by the almost sacred significance of the place. He pondered on the months spent here by Franklin and his men that fateful winter before being swallowed up by the mysterious Arctic mists the following spring, never to be heard from again.

What had strongly attracted Amundsen to the Arctic was the possibility of being the first to navigate the Northwest Passage, but to impart respectability and attract funding to his scheme, he had announced a valid scientific goal. That goal was the accurate updating of the position of the ever-wandering north magnetic pole which had first been located by James Clark Ross[12] in 1831. He never lost track of that goal. Happily for him, it turned out that the pursuit of both goals were completely compatible. The direction to the north magnetic pole as suggested by readings Amundsen took at Beechey Island appeared to point him serendipitously southwest, right down Peel Sound and the Northwest Passage. But first, Beechey Island was to be explored.

Northumberland House was the name of a structure built on Beechey in 1852 by Commander W.J.S. Pullen to house a cache of food and equipment for the subsequent Sir Edward Belcher expedition sent out in search of Franklin. After Belcher failed to find Franklin, and was on his way home to England, he left the building and whatever remained of provisions and equipment there for the lost explorer in case he might pass by and be in need of them. Many searchers and explorers had landed at Beechey in succeeding years, finding the cache seriously deteriorating with time. In 1903, when Amundsen landed there, the cache had been so completely ruined by the years and the resident bears that there was hardly anything usable left. Amundsen did take away a bit of remaining coal, though, and some shoe leather that had survived intact for a half century and that was in fact preferred by the *Gjøa*'s crew to the "best American sole leather" they had brought with them.

Over time, Beechey Island has become a memorial for those who had perished in their efforts to push back the frontiers of discovery and knowledge of the mysterious Arctic. The first monument to be erected was a tall column as a cenotaph in honour of those who died during the Belcher expedition. This was followed by a marble tablet brought in by Sir Leopold McClintock on behalf of Lady Jane Franklin in memory of her husband and his crew, and placed at the foot of the Belcher column in 1858. On the column itself is attached a tablet in honour of French Lieutenant Joseph René Bellot, who was drowned in these waters and from whom Bellot Strait, which separates Somerset Island from Boothia Peninsula, takes its name. All these memorials together with the four, and perhaps five, graves of Arctic mariners, plus the absolute barrenness of Beechey Island make it a place steeped in death. Before rowing out to the *Gjøa* for the last time, Amundsen left a record of their progress to date in a tin can that he hung on the Belcher column in a conspicuous location. This record was found the following year, 1904, by A.P. Low[13] on his Canadian expedition of claiming Arctic islands for Canada. Low removed the record and later forwarded it to the Norwegian government to inform them of Amundsen's progress.

> With the departure from Beechey, a new chapter opened in our expedition. We now knew the course we were to take; the die was cast, and we had only to push on and make headway. Our voyage now assumed a new

character. Hitherto we had been sailing in safe and known waters, where many others had preceded us. Now we were making our way through waters never sailed in, save possibly by a couple of vessels, and were hoping to reach even farther where no keel had ever plowed. We were very sanguine.

At midday on August 24, *Gjøa* and her crew of seven left Beechey Island and sailed down Peel Sound heading toward Franklin Strait, two bodies of water that separate Somerset Island and Boothia Peninsula from Prince of Wales Island. Rare was the ship, if any, that had had such an easy time of it from the point of view of ice and storms in these waters. The year 1903 appears to have been exceptional in the Arctic for its relative freedom from ice, and for its peaceful conditions.

The expected, but much feared ice finally did make its appearance after the *Gjøa* had sailed south down Peel Sound almost one-third the length of the coast of Somerset Island. The direct sun glaring in their eyes, combined with its flickering reflection from the shore-to-shore ice, convinced the crew that they had finally reached a solid barrier of ice that would seriously impede their progress. As the ship approached the seemingly solid blockade, it turned out to be only an optical illusion created by the sun shining and sparkling off the surface of water with broken-up ice floating in it. This was no problem at all, especially since there were quite navigable clear channels on either side of the ice. Amundsen and his crew were soon happily sailing in open waters past tiny Prescott Island, having suffered nothing more than a bit of anxiety.

Headed south through open water, the *Gjøa* entered Franklin Strait on the evening of the same day and found that navigation suddenly became a lot more difficult. From that point on, the ship's magnetic compass lost its capacity to accurately point toward the magnetic north pole due to the proximity of that natural phenomenon. Wrote Amundsen, "We were thus reduced to steering by the stars, like our forefathers the Vikings." This was a significant challenge to the safety of the ship and her crew, especially as two-thirds of the time the sky was thickly veiled by fog and sights of heavenly bodies could not be

taken. The *Gjøa* was fast approaching the point that marked the farthest a ship had ever penetrated into the Northwest Passage when, in
1874, Sir Allen Young in the *Pandora* met an absolute blockade of ice
there that put an end to his progress.[14] At this point, Amundsen admitted to a certain nervous concern over the potential fate of his
expedition should it meet a similar blockade of ice as well, but he kept
these thoughts to himself.

Quite suddenly, Amundsen felt an unusual lurching movement
under him as he walked the deck, although the sea around him was
calm. Caught by surprise, he stopped, with all his senses on the alert,
but the movement was gone. He dismissed this passing feeling as
some nervous reaction on his part caused by the tension of the situation and continued walking. But it came again, and again he had to
dismiss it as a strange and inexplicable sensation since there was
absolutely nothing that he could see in his surrounding environment
that could account for it. But when it occurred a third time, he finally
and suddenly realized what its source was, and welcomed it with
supreme pleasure. The *Gjøa* was rolling slightly with an almost imper-
ceptible ocean swell, which could only mean one thing – that
Amundsen's ship was facing open water to the south. There was to be
no ice barrier! By then his crewmembers began noticing the increasing swell too, and it was smiles all around, for they also know what it
meant. The news could not have been better. "...this swell, at this place
and time – it was not a delight, it was a rapture that filled me to the
soul," wrote Amundsen.

For the next few days, Amundsen conned his ship southward without benefit of compass, losing time when *Gjøa* inadvertently got stuck
in an ice field, got unstuck and finally continued, going steadily south
through the Northwest Passage toward James Ross Strait. Amundsen
was now navigating by dead reckoning because his compass was useless and he could not see land for the dull weather. He knew that he was
passing in the vicinity of Cape Adelaide Regina, but he could not see it.
This particular spot held significance for Amundsen as James Clark
Ross had determined the north magnetic pole to be located there in
1831. Finding out where this pole had migrated to since 1831 was one of

his major objectives on this trip, one which he would address as soon as he could locate a suitable harbour to anchor the *Gjøa* in for the winter.

On September 1 at eight o'clock in the morning, Amundsen retired to his bunk after a night of navigating as best he could in the darkness and without a compass, only to be roughly awakened by a violent shock at three hours later that brought him topside in a flash. The *Gjøa* had run aground amidships on a shoal just off the Beaufort Islands, well stuck for the time being, but not too seriously as things turned out. All sail was set and the engine was started at full speed, which was enough to get the vessel off the shoal, losing just a few splinters from the false keel. Fortunately, she was still tight and the pumps were not needed.

As Amundsen sat below decks that night entering the day's events in his journal, a terrific shriek rent the air which "...thrilled me to the very marrow – something extraordinary had happened." It was indeed an event that very nearly put an end to the expedition. A huge plume of flame and billows of thick smoke leapt skywards from the engine-room skylight – an engine room that was lined with several metal tanks full of fuel. The situation was critical. Everyone knew the potential outcome of the blaze if it was not controlled immediately. The whole expedition could very well be vaporized in a huge explosion and fireball, becoming famous as yet another mysterious Arctic disappearance. The crew grabbed the ship's two fire extinguishers, emptied them into the engine room and furiously dumped bucket after bucket of sea water on the fire before they brought the raging flames under control. It had been a close call indeed – how close Amundsen and his crew did not know until they analyzed the cause of the near disaster.

Spontaneous combustion among some oil-saturated cleaning rags carelessly left on top of the fuel tanks was suspected as the cause of the fire. Just before the flames erupted though, something had happened that could have meant the end of them all. One of the fuel tanks in the engine room had been reported as leaking. Amundsen lost no time in ordering that tank drained into another empty tank, and Ristvedt lost no time in carrying out the order. In the frantic fight to put out the fire a short time later, the tap of the now empty tank that leaked had been accidentally knocked off. Had Ristvedt not emptied it promptly on

Amundsen's orders, over 450 litres (100 gallons) of fuel would have gushed out into the flaming engine room during the fire. "I need not enlarge on what would have been the inevitable sequel," Amundsen reported laconically in his book *The North West Passage*. The lesson learned from promptly carrying out orders was not lost on Ristvedt and the rest of the crew. Had he delayed in draining the leaking tank into another empty one, no one would have had to worry about ever carrying out another order, promptly or otherwise.

At four o'clock in the morning of September 2, Amundsen left behind a day of extreme stress and potentially deadly events to continue southward through James Ross Strait, heading toward Rae Strait and, unknowingly, toward another day of thrilling, life-threatening adventure. At eleven in the morning, gale-force winds made it necessary for Amundsen to seek shelter behind a low island where the *Gjøa* spent the rest of the day and night at anchor.

Early next morning at four a.m., the *Gjøa* sailed on after weathering the gale for some sixteen hours at anchor. It wasn't long before she ran into trouble again as Amundsen tried to get around Matty Island. Unwittingly, the *Gjøa* had become enmeshed in a region of submerged shallow reefs between Boothia Peninsula and Matty Island. Although her captain thought he had sailed far enough away from the shoals to avoid them, the *Gjøa* ran aground on a shallow rock but just as quickly slipped off. Some minutes later the ship struck again, once more got off, and then hung up for good. Amundsen stopped the engine and scrambled up to the crow's nest to peer into the clear water and evaluate the situation. It did not look good. At first, aft looked like the shortest way to go to get free of the submerged rock, but upon close examination,

Amundsen realized that the shoals behind them, that they had struck just a few minutes before, were in shallower water than the rock they were presently stuck on. The only way out seemed to be forward, but that was far from encouraging.

> The soundings gave us little hope. The reef shallowed
> up in that direction, and had not more than a fathom

A painting of the *Gjøa* making its way through the rocks. *From* The North West Passage *by Roald Amundsen.*

[six feet] upon it in the shallowest part. Taking the shortest way ahead, the distance across the reef was about 220 yards. With a few tons of ballast the Gjøa had a draft of six feet. Loaded as she was, she drew 10 feet 2 inches. The prospect of getting across was therefore not brilliant, but we had no choice. We were compelled to lighten the vessel as much as possible.

The cases of deck cargo that had been so painstakingly loaded aboard at Dalrymple Rock now had to be tossed overboard if the ship was to survive. First the crew jettisoned 25 of their heaviest cases of dog pemmican. Now they would have to hunt or fish, or both, to feed their dogs. Then all the cases of deck cargo on one side of the ship were cast overboard to make the ship heel over on the opposite side in an attempt to make it easier for the ship to slide off the reef. She had grounded at high tide, so as the tide fell, there was no use trying to get her off the rock. The men did everything possible to lighten the ship in preparation for the next high water. A kedge anchor was rowed out in the *Gjøa's* boat and set down to the south of the ship. A kedge is an anchor that is thrown down to the sea bottom some distance ahead in the direction a ship wants to go, as a leverage point against which the crew attempts to winch their vessel. At seven in the evening, high tide floated the ship higher, but no amount of effort could budge her of the rock. At eight o'clock all efforts were abandoned.

The next morning Amundsen came up on deck at two a.m. to find that a fresh wind was blowing from the north, the best direction possible for his purposes:

> At 3 A.M. the vessel began to move as if in convolutions. I had all hands called up so as to be ready to avail ourselves of any chance that might present itself. The north wind freshened to a gale accompanied by sleet. We hove on the kedge, time after time, but to no purpose. The vessel pitched violently. I took counsel with my comrades as I always did in critical situations, and we decided as a last resource, to try and get her off with the sails. The spray was dashing over the ship, and the wind came in gusts, howling through the rigging, but we struggled and toiled and got the sails set. Then we commenced a method of sailing not one of us is ever likely to forget even should he attain the age of Methuselah. The mighty press of sail and the high choppy sea, combined, had the effect of lifting the vessel up, and pitching her forward again amongst the rocks, so that we expected every moment to see her planks scattered on the sea. The false keel was splintered and floated up. All we could do was watch the course of events and calmly await the issue.... I had to hold fast with all my strength whenever the vessel, after being lifted, pitched down onto the rocks, or I should have been flung into the sea.... The water on the reef got shallower, and I noted how the water broke on the outer edge. It looked as if the raging north wind meant to carry us just to that bitter

end. The sails were as taught as drumheads, the rigging trembled, and I expected it to go overboard every minute. We were steadily approaching the shallowest part of the reef, and sharper and sharper grew the lash of the spray over the vessel.

I thought it almost impossible the ship could hold together if she could get on the outer edge of the reef, which in fact, was almost lying dry. There was still time to let down a boat and load it with the most indispensable necessaries. I stood up there, in the most terrible agony, struggling for a decision. On me rested every responsibility, and the moment came when I had to make my choice – to abandon the Gjøa, take to the boats, and let her be smashed up, or to dare the worst, and perchance go to meet death with all souls onboard...' We will clear the boats and load them with provisions, rifles and ammunition.' Then Lund, who was standing nearest, asked whether we might not make a last attempt by casting the remainder of the deck cargo overboard. This was, my own secret ardent desire, to which I had not dared to yield, for the sake of the others. Now, all with one accord agreed with Lund, and hey-presto! we went for the deck cargo. We set to in pairs, and cases of 4 cwt. were flung over the rail like trusses of hay. This done, up I climbed into the rigging again. There was not more than a boat's length between the shallowest part and us. The spray and sleet were washing over the vessel, the mast trembled, and the Gjøa seemed to pull herself together for a final last leap. She was lifted up high and flung bodily on to the bare rocks, bump, bump – with terrific force.... In my distress I sent up (I honestly confess it) an ardent prayer to the Almighty. Yet another thump, worse than ever, then one more, and we slid off.

The *Gjøa* was finally free of the clawing rocky shoals, but she was not out of the woods yet. There were still rocks all around her and conning the ship visually from the crow's nest was absolutely essential if she wasn't to be left high and dry again. Amundsen called down his steering orders from above to Lieutenant Hansen at the wheel. "There is something wrong with the rudder, it will not steer," Hansen screamed up to Amundsen in the crow's nest. At that very moment, the *Gjøa* pitched again as she was swept over yet another rocky crest. "The rudder is all right again," shouted Hansen. Amundsen later wrote, "A most wonderful thing had happened..."

The rudder was hung by two vertical iron pins one above the other that drop through two corresponding iron eyelets just like farmers' gates are still hung today. In crashing around on rocky shoals, the rudder had been lifted up and the two pins had come out of their eyelets, effectively making the rudder a free body, ready to drop into the sea. By the sheerest stroke of good luck, the last bump on a rocky crest had lifted the rudder again and dropped it back into its proper position with the pins engaged in the eyelets. The crew broke out in unrestrained jubilation. Wonderful indeed!

From that point on, the *Gjøa* did not sail without a man guiding her helmsman from the crow's nest and another on deck heaving the lead (pronounced like the metal it is) line to measure the distance to the sea floor. Amundsen had learned his lesson. The *Gjøa* sailed east away from the shoals and closer to the coast of Boothia Peninsula looking for deeper water, which she found. She was firmly anchored in five fathoms (nine metres/thirty feet) to give the crew some recovery time from the terror, excitement and mental strain of the preceding hours, and also to permit various repairs necessitated by all the rough treatment the ship had undergone. Some of the crew rowed to shore to carry out various duties. It must have felt really good to plant their feet on the solid dry land of Boothia.

Amundsen deposited a report in a cairn that was built up out of the surrounding rocks. The geologist took his observations and collected various fossils while the hunters sighted some caribou. Amundsen walked around and found a good number of old tent rings where Inuit had camped. When darkness came on, the shore party rowed back to the ship where one man stood watch and the rest went to sleep for much needed rest. At 11 o'clock, the watch reported a stiff breeze blowing from the south. There was only one thing to do – batten down the hatches and make sure the anchors were well secured. In the rising wind, Amundsen feared the anchor chains might part, a breakage that would have disastrous consequences. The engine was kept working full speed ahead to relieve the strain on the anchor chains. A wooden boat and a number of canvas boats were filled with provisions in the extreme case the crew had to abandon ship. Gale winds swept in from various directions for five days and nights while the crew waited uneasily for calm to return. Finally, at four o'clock in the morning on the 8th of September, the crew was able to weigh anchor and continue on their way under a fair northwest wind.

Amundsen crossed Rae Strait to the west closer to the shore of King William Island where he found deeper water. As the *Gjøa* approached land, Hansen who was in the crow's nest sang out, "I see the finest little harbour in the world." Amundsen could not see it at deck level so he climbed up to join Hansen and sure enough there looked to be a jewel of a protected haven of rest for the *Gjøa*, her captain and his weary crew. Had Amundsen's primary objective been to navigate through the Northwest Passage, he probably would have continued on since Simpson Strait to the west appeared ice free. But there were two reasons why he did not. Firstly, winter was coming on apace and Gjøahavn, as he named the natural harbour, was really an ideal, protected cove in which to overwinter his ship. Secondly, it was also perfect from the point of view of distance from the north magnetic pole, which appeared to be about 145 kilometres (90 miles) away. For making magnetic measurements, he could not get too close to the pole. As Amundsen put it, a distance of 90 miles "should, according to the dicta of scientific men, be particularly suited for a fixed magnetic station."

Amundsen and his crew spent the next couple of days carefully exploring Gjøahavn by rowboat to make sure it was safe to bring their ship into the natural harbour. He found that the narrow entrance was barely wide enough for two ships to pass each other, but the average depth was six fathoms (11 metres/36 feet) and that was plenty. Drinking water was available and caribou tracks were in abundance. The harbour was all that could be desired. At 7:30 p.m. on Saturday, September 12, the wind died down enough to allow the *Gjøa* to enter under engine power, and at 8:30 she was anchored in her berth for the winter – in fact for the next 23 months – on the southeast corner of King William Island. Amundsen's goal of sailing through the Northwest Passage was put on the back burner for the time being while his alternative objective – pinning down the north magnetic pole – took centre stage.

CHAPTER FOUR

History of the
North Magnetic Pole

THE EARLY NINETEENTH CENTURY WAS AN
exciting period in the history of magnetism. Interest in finding a sailing route through the Arctic islands, the so-called Northwest Passage,
led to the British Royal Navy sending numerous expeditions to the
Canadian Arctic. Because of its importance to navigation, the Royal
Navy was also interested in magnetism and thus included magnetic
observers on many of its expeditions, the most notable being Edward
Sabine and James Clark Ross.

By 1829 sufficient magnetic observations had been made in the
Canadian Arctic to restrict the location of the North Magnetic Pole to a
hitherto unexplored section of the central Arctic. At this point the
British Admiralty suddenly lost interest in Arctic exploration. However,
John Ross (the uncle of James Clark Ross) was able to obtain sponsor-
ship from the wealthy British distiller Felix Booth, for another attempt
at the Northwest Passage – one that would go through the uncharted
territory in which the north magnetic pole was thought to be. John

Ross's expedition was remarkable in many ways. His ship, the *Victory*, was powered by steam. This first attempt to use steam power in the Arctic caused expedition leader Ross to write, "there seems indeed no end to the vexation produced by this accursed machinery..."[15]

James Clark Ross was well aware that the ship's route down the east coast of Boothia Peninsula brought it very close to the magnetic pole, and observations made while the ship lay imprisoned in the ice of the Gulf of Boothia confirmed that the pole lay no more than a couple of hundred kilometres or sixty miles to the west. In May 1831, Ross led a small party overland, and on the last day of the month reached a spot on the west coast of Boothia Peninsula (70° 5' 17" N, 96° 46' 45" W) where he believed the north magnetic pole should be. After carrying out a lengthy series of observations in an abandoned igloo, Ross computed a magnetic inclination of 89° 59'. Given the accuracy of his instruments, and the variable nature of the magnetic field, he could legitimately claim to be at the pole. In his uncle's book on the expedition, James Clark Ross wrote "it almost seemed as if we had accomplished everything that we had come so far to see and to do; as if our voyage and all its labours were at an end and that nothing now remained for us but to return home and be happy for the rest of our days."[16]

However, returning home was more complicated than anticipated. The expedition was forced to spend four winters in the Arctic due to the imprisonment of the *Victory* in the ice. Eventually, the crew abandoned the ship and reached the north coast of Baffin Island in lifeboats where they were rescued. In four years only three men were lost, a remarkable feat of Arctic survival for the time.

CHAPTER FIVE

The Gjøa's First Winter, 1903–04

THE FIRST ORDER OF AMUNDSEN'S BUSINESS IN Gjøahavn was to plan the living arrangements for the seven men and then, to execute the plan. Two men would live on shore, Wiik and Ristvedt. The other five would live on board ship in two separate quarters. Amundsen and Lieutenant Hansen lived together in the so-called cabin aft of the main mast, while Lund, Helmer Hansen and Lindstrøm lived in the fo'c'sle.[17] In addition, Lindstrøm, the cook, would ply his culinary skills from a new location for his galley – the hold. To create adequate room for these arrangements, it was decided to remove all the provisions from the ship and to store them in a provisions shed built on shore for that purpose. The explosive guncotton was wisely located quite some distance away from anything else in a small explosives shed. Unloading had to take place before the sea ice immobilized the ship in its frozen embrace. The Gjøa was anchored as close to shore as possible and an aerial rope way was built from mid-mast to an anchor on shore. Cases were offloaded by sliding them to shore in

The *Gjøa* iced in for the winter at Gjøahavn. *From* The North West Passage *by Roald Amundsen.*

right smart fashion down a pulley system. After unloading was finished, the ship was distanced some 50 metres (165 feet) offshore and solidly anchored there until the ice locked her in for the winter. By the 3rd of October, the men were able to walk over the ice from ship to shore. Winter was seriously setting in.

Two substantial buildings were built on shore, one as home to Wiik and Ristvedt for almost two years, and the other to house the continuously recording instruments for measuring magnetic variation, or declination from true north. Another magnetic parameter – absolute magnetic force – would be monitored in a specially designed snow house. Magnetic variation, or declination, is a constantly varying quantity that changes on an hourly, daily, monthly, and yearly basis. As can be guessed, its measurement had to take place far from any source of man-made magnetic influence. All metal used in building the magnetic variation house had to be copper, including nails. It also had to be built on a solid foundation so that the instruments for measuring magnetic variation would not be affected by physical vibrations. The *Gjøa*'s cargo included a number of slabs of marble on which to mount these sensitive instruments.

The construction design of these two substantial houses was testimony to Amundsen's forethought in planning the expedition. All the equipment and provisions had been packed in waterproof metal cases, which in turn were fitted into cubical wooden boxes made of carefully selected, quality wood to protect them. When these cases were offloaded into the storage shed on shore, the outer wooden boxes were removed and carefully set aside. They became available for construction purposes. Filled with sand, they became building blocks with which to build the walls of the two substantial houses, and a fine, solid building material they were.

When the snow came, the two last buildings required would be built of snow blocks, one to protect the observatory for absolute magnetic measurements, which were a measure of the strength of the magnetic force at that location, and the other for the astronomical observatory to take star sightings.

Two important items still had to be addressed before it got too cold – stockpiling meat for men and dogs, and making sure the men had enough adequate clothing to withstand the deep and bitter cold of the dark season to come. Luckily, both these requirements were satisfied by one thing – caribou. These animals had already started migrating from King William Island, where they had spent the summer in lush surroundings, to the Canadian mainland where the winter forage was more abundant. But alas for the caribou, wolves were also more abundant on the mainland. The caribou had been free of these predators for the summer as the wolves had not followed them onto Prince William Island the previous spring.

The caribou were not difficult to find. One day a herd of 50 almost walked into camp, led by a splendid buck with magnificently huge antlers. They walked single file along the crest of a ridge above Gjøahavn, crossed over to the other side and disappeared without detecting the scent of man because of a wind favouring the hunters, who didn't have to be asked to swing into action. Rifles appeared as if by magic and off they went in hot pursuit. Amundsen himself was not a hunter, so he gave himself the job of bringing the game in by dog team. That work was not easy for him because he, like everybody else, had had precious little experience with driving dogs up to that point.

Hunting was not easy on King William Island, a flat land devoid of any high vegetation or rocks behind which hunters could hide. The movement of stalkers is perceptible at long distances to caribou eyes, and appears as very threatening to them. It is only when the animals' attention is distracted by some occupation such as grazing is it possible creep up on them, if one were stealthy enough. When caribou stop eating and lie down for a rest, it is virtually impossible to get close enough to them to get within shooting distance. The hunter then has two choices – give up, or lie down as well, and wait for the animals to resume grazing; and the wind had better be in the right direction. It may literally take hours for a hunter to get into shooting position. Inuit have been much better in developing patience for this kind of game then white men.

At other times during that first winter in Gjøahavn, herd after herd of caribou passed by the harbour, so despite the skill required, the ship's crew had no trouble getting meat. Between the caribou and the plentiful ptarmigan, the men ate well. On October 8, 1903, Hansen set a hunting record that was not beaten in the two winters spent at Gjøahavn. He returned from a short hunt one day with thirteen caribou kills to his credit. Before the men could set out with dog teams to fetch the carcasses, a doe and two calves came walking into the little village of buildings and paid for their curiosity with their lives. Food was certainly not a problem.

By mid-October, enough snow had fallen and it had been sufficiently compacted by the wind that Amundsen and his crew were able to cut out snow blocks for building the two last structures required to protect the observatory for absolute magnetic observations, and for the meteorological observatory. One can get an idea of how hard snow can become when compacted by Arctic wind from the average weight of the building blocks – some weighed 90 kilograms (200 pounds) each.

One late October morning, something happened that Amundsen and his crew had started doubting would ever come to pass. As usual, the men were standing on the fo'c'sle after breakfast keeping watch on the hillside for caribou when someone pointed to the north and cried out, "Here is more sport!" The hunters jumped to get their rifles, but Hansen, who had particularly sharp eyes, stood rooted to his spot, unmoving. Someone asked, "Well, Hansen, have you no mind to shoot reindeer today?" "Ah yes," he replied, "but not that sort of reindeer, over there – they walk on two legs!" At this startling announcement, Amundsen rushed below deck to fetch his binoculars and confirmed what sharp-eyed Hansen had seen; there were five men.[18]

"Eskimo!"

Amundsen and his crew had often talked about the possibility of meeting Inuit, but it was now the end of October and there had been no sign of them except some very old tent rings formed by rocks used to hold down the skins of a tent, so the Norwegians had concluded the Inuit were probably "extinct" in that region. They were utterly pleased and excited to see that was not the case.

Although the explorers were excited at this meeting of the races, they were also apprehensive about how to approach these people of such vastly different culture from theirs. Amundsen knew "from old books of travel in these regions that the North American Eskimo were not always amicably disposed." He had also read that *Teima* (or *Taima* as it is written today) was a good word to use in such encounters because he thought it meant "a right hearty good day," which is not an accurate translation, although it is not a bad word to know as it is often used by Inuit in an all-purpose, positive way. Amundsen decided the best approach was to consider that the Inuit might possibly be hostile and to arm himself and the two other members of the welcoming committee, Hansen and Lund, with loaded rifles, hoping for the best but prepared for the worst. The two parties walked towards each other, without a doubt, with trepidation in both camps. The Inuit were now some 500 metres distant and approaching the vessel. About halfway there, they halted, as did the three Norwegians who stood in a semi-military stance to dispel any signs of weakness. The Inuit presented a less than threatening behaviour as they stood there "talking excitedly, pointing with their hands, laughing and gesticulating, without any noticeable indication of hostility," but then they started advancing again toward the three white strangers in a way that Amundsen interpreted as, if not hostile, at least not confidence-inspiring either.

> And on we marched, expecting every moment to see
> the enemy take their bows from their backs and level

an arrow at us. But no! evidently they are of a different mind. Is this a ruse? Suddenly there flashed through my mind, heated with the excitement of warfare, the word 'Teima!' and 'Teima' I shout with all the power of my lusty lungs. But now our excitement can no longer be restrained, we must bring matters to a crisis, and we rush forward ready for action. Then I hear the call: 'Manik-tu-mi! Manik-tu-mi!' And this has quite a familiar sound – I well remember it from McClintock – it is the Eskimo's friendliest greeting. In a moment we fling away our rifles and hasten toward our friends, and with the universal shout of 'Manik-tu-mi! Manik-tu-mi!' we embrace and pat each other, and it would be hard to say on which side the joy is greater.

Amundsen was quite impressed by the physical appearance of his newfound friends. He found some of them handsome and compared them favourably with the people he had met in Northern Greenland. They were tall and muscular in the eyes of the Norwegian leader.

The Inuit accepted an invitation to visit the ship with obvious pleasure. There were 100 carcasses lying on deck, which obviously attracted the visitors' attention, since they stared at them, but their deeper emotions were not evident. That much available meat at the same time and place for just seven men must surely have impressed these bow-and-arrow hunters. Inuit and Norwegians spent a long time together, "talking, laughing and joking," wrote Amundsen, but it was surely the body language rather than the spoken word that gave any meaning to the "conversations." As good hosts, the Norwegians offered their guests coffee and ships' biscuits, but these did not very much gratify the Inuit palate. Water to drink, though, made them light up with delight. On a hunch, Amundsen offered them a leg of meat from the carcass pile and this the Inuit knew what to do with. They immediately pulled out long knives from the legs of their *kamiks* (Inuit footgear) and fell to it until only bones were left. Two other legs of caribou offered to them suffered the same fate. Amundsen had not realized to what extent his visitors were still armed.

Faces of young women were tattooed to enhance their appearance. Kabloka, from Gjøahavn, was considered a beauty. *From* The North West Passage *by Roald Amundsen.*

Two members of the crew were not present at these exciting events – Ristvedt and Wiik, who were working in their house on shore. Amundsen decided to pay them a visit to introduce them to their new Inuit friends. The two shore-dwellers jumped up with great surprise at the sight of the Inuit and enthusiastically joined the celebrations. Hearty laughter rang out over the hills of Gjøahavn, the Inuit contributing tremendous roars to the cacophony. The visitors stayed overnight and went back home the next day only to return a couple of days later with some caribou skins for the Norwegians with which to make winter clothes. These essential items were welcome indeed to Amundsen and his men.

The Norwegians decided to accompany the Inuit back to their home to see where and how they lived. Amundsen understood from their guests that they would not sleep on the trip back home, so he concluded that it could not be far away. In the early afternoon, darkness was approaching and Amundsen thought they had better get a move on while it was still light out. What the captain of the *Gjøa* had not learned yet was that the Inuit travelled with great indifference as to whether it was light or dark, and were not unduly inconvenienced by fog, snowstorm or wind. By 3:30 in the afternoon, with darkness setting in, the travellers reached the top of a hill from which they could see lights in the distance below in a snug, sheltered valley. By the time

A young Inuit man, known as the "Owl," demonstrates his hunting technique with bow and arrow. *From* The North West Passage *by Roald Amundsen.*

they reached the Inuit camp, it was quite dark. Upon hearing the cries of the arriving Inuit, those in camp swarmed toward the travellers to meet them. There followed a scene that Amundsen would never forget: "I was surrounded by a crowd of savages yelling and shouting one above the other, staring into my face, grabbing at my clothes, stroking and feeling me."

By this time, he was ready for some rest, warmth and food. Amundsen followed Attira, an Inuit who had impressed him, into his igloo, which was one of six built around a large lake the Inuit called *Kaa-aak-ka*. The igloo was a large structure and was home to Attira and Tamoktuktu plus the children of the two families, a total of eight people in spacious accommodations.

> Soon after our arrival, the male members of the colony assembled for a feast consisting of raw reindeer meat and water. Three entire carcasses of reindeer disappeared before I could consume a sandwich. They were chatting and laughing all the time. But there could not have been any efficient 'Women's Rights' Association here, as none of the women were present at the feast. When I tried to show them how we conducted ourselves towards our women, and courteously offered some

meat to Mrs. Tamoktuktu, they shrieked with laughter, and evidently considered that I was a most irrational being. When the men had eaten their fill, the women were admitted. The greeted me with 'manik-tu-mi,' and stroked me all over the body. Then they departed without having been offered any food. I was subsequently set at ease on this point, being informed that even Eskimo women are not unmindful of their own bodily wants when left to themselves. The disappearance of a joint of reindeer causes no particular comment.

At about 10 p.m. Amundsen went to bed in his sleeping bag, laid out between the two families on the common, elevated sleeping platform of packed snow. He fell into a deep sleep until broad daylight, which at that season in those latitudes was not early. He awoke to a scene of naked Inuit sitting upright in bed enjoying their morning air bath. However, he did not participate in the ritual, preferring to hunker back down into the warmth of his sleeping bag to catch another forty winks. Later that afternoon, the leader of the Norwegian expedition was back at Gjøahavn having spent an exciting and fascinating interlude with people of an unbelievably different culture. This was the beginning of a two-year happy relationship.

It was not long before Inuit came to visit the *Gjøa* on a regular basis and a village of igloos sprang up around the ship, housing some two hundred men, women and children. "This was an opportunity to delight the soul of an anthropologist and ethnographer," remarked Amundsen. He had prepared beforehand for just such an occurrence by having on board many objects for barter.

> I set about to acquire a complete set of museum exhibits to illustrate every phase of the life of the Eskimo.... I got samples of literally everything these Eskimos possessed, from suits of clothing worn by both sexes, young and old, to samples of every kind of

implement they had for cooking, sledding, and the chase.... To me it was wonderful to see the artistic sense and fabricating skill evidenced in garments. The women are very adept at cutting out the black parts and the white parts of the caribou skins and fashioning them into beautiful shapes and then working these parts of skins into elaborate patterns. Their bead work, too, made from the teeth and bits of dried bone of the caribou, showed taste and skill.

Imagine, too, the interest I took in the implements used by these people. Their skill in taking the bones of freshly killed game and stretching and twisting them while still green into proper lengths and shapes from which to fashion spear heads and shaft needles for sewing, and other useful articles, was to me a fascinating example of human ingenuity.

Some of these trades may sound like hard bargains on our part, but this was not the case. The Eskimos traded us only of their surplus for things of our stock, which to them were of equal value. A hunting knife of fine Swedish steel could easily be worth to an Eskimo hunter far more than a dozen beautiful furs for which he had no present need and which he could easily duplicate... It was a perfect example of a good bargain, in which both sides profited.

When Amundsen saw that the Inuit had established semi-permanent family residences at Gjøahavn, he thought it best to put his men on notice about a delicate subject. Most of the Inuit had never seen a white man before. Seventy-two years before, in 1831, their grandfathers had only briefly met James Clark Ross and his men when they had arrived overland in search of the position of the north magnetic pole. The Inuit at Gjøahavn in 1903, however, had never seen these "godlike white men," only heard about them through their parents and grandparents. To the 1903 Inuit, though, Amundsen and his men had

Young Nechilli archers –
prospective hunters.
From The North West
Passage *by Roald Amundsen.*

some of the same attributes of gods as Ross and his men. Only divine beings could possess such powerful and mysterious weapons, magical devices for making instant fire and light, and so much useful equipment. It was to the Norwegians' advantage with respect to their safety, that the Inuit remain under that impression. The one thing that could most quickly destroy these illusions, according to Amundsen, was if his men should yield to their "baser passions." He believed that if his crew took liberties with Inuit women, white men would fall to the level of mere men in the eyes of the Inuit and put themselves at their mercy. "I therefore took the first opportunity to have a most serious talk with my companions and urge them not to yield to this kind of temptation."

Amundsen was well aware that desire for companionship can exercise tremendous power over men in the circumstances the crew of the *Gjøa* found themselves, but one has to wonder if he underestimated the power this desire had over himself. According to a northern publication called *Above & Beyond*: "Indeed, there are a few people in Gjoa Haven today who are proud to declare that they are Roald Amundsen's grandchildren, including Paul Iqalluq who is quoted as saying, 'My father was the son of Amundsen... I'm one of the proudest people in Gjoa Haven.' "[19]

Dogs are absolutely essential for anyone travelling during the cold season in the Arctic, be they Inuit or otherwise. But dogs come with a price. They require an enormous quantity of food each day and they will devour almost anything in reach, be it edible or not. They are messy and leave their mess anywhere and everywhere, and they can be dangerous for other dogs and at times even for humans. The expedition had already lost some dogs to disease early on and now in November two more died. Amundsen concluded, rightly or wrongly, that lack of fat in their diet was the culprit. The caribou killed that year had remarkably little fat on them and there was precious little to keep men healthy, let alone dogs. One day Amundsen's dogs helped themselves to a meal that he qualified as "unexpected as it was unpleasant." A bitch named Silla that was highly pregnant had been confined on shore until she produced her offspring, but she managed to escape from her prison and headed immediately for the ship. She was halfway there when an escort of her excited suitors met her. Silla had not quite made it to the safety of the vessel when the crucial moment arrived and four little pups fell wriggling to the snow. As if at a signal, all the waiting dogs rushed at the pups and four succeeded in each ravenously gobbling one down. Silla continued walking toward the ship when she was once more seized with labour pains, and with a couple of convulsions, gave birth to a fifth pup. Lest the other dogs eat it, she jumped on it and devoured it herself, and a strange, sad peace descended upon the canine colony.

December with its long, dark days fell upon the tiny *Gjøa* and her seven lone sailors lost in the vast wilderness of one of the most inhospitable regions of the world. The long-awaited celebration of Christmas brought not only much needed merriment, but also loneliness and sadness at the thoughts of their loved ones back home celebrating the very same Christmas, but in a much warmer and more congenial atmosphere, surrounded by family and friends. Such thoughts had best remain fleeting under such conditions or they risk causing a descent into destructive melancholy. In fact, Christmas day 1903 was a double celebration – it was not only Christmas, but also Gustav Wiik's twenty-fifth birthday. Lindstrøm the cook was the busiest man of all at this season and his culinary magic was essential to the proper celebration of this most important of feasts. The cook was hard at work these days and his responsibilities were heavy. On him rested the task of satisfying

Celebrating the first Christmas Eve on board the *Gjøa*, 1903. *From* The North West Passage *by Roald Amundsen.*

his demanding clients. He baked and broiled for hours at a time, producing mountains of delicacies, which he had to be very careful to hide, for his clients, were not above devouring his dishes ahead of time if they were not well concealed.

A Christmas tree was fashioned out of glazed and reflective paper illuminated by flaming candles. Family and friends of the crew had brought gifts on board for several Christmases. They were clearly marked, "Do not open before December 25, 1903, 1904 and 1905." Otherwise, in their thirst for things from home, the men might have opened them all at once, carried away in an orgy of Christmas spirit. On Christmas Eve, there was a beautiful aurora borealis decorating the night sky, arching its huge ever-shifting veil of light over Gjøahavn, the tiny craft and her crew that she protected.

Once the excitement of Christmas and New Year's over, Amundsen began planning a dogsled trip north, back up the part of the Northwest Passage that had caused the *Gjøa* so much grief the previous fall. He wanted to make magnetic observations near Matty Island as part of a network of observations in different locations for zeroing in on where the magnetic north pole had shifted to since Ross' time. His plan was then to push farther north to the Tasmania Islands for more magnetic observations, and finally on to Port Leopold on the northern tip of Somerset Island. Port Leopold was frequently visited by whaling vessels and was a place where mail could be left for the whalers to take

back to Europe. It was also a place where a Danish whaler was supposed to have left a depot of supplies for the *Gjøa* as prearranged by
Amundsen.

The first stage of this trip would consist of a ferry of two sled loads
of food and supplies to a convenient point some days north of Gjøahavn,
where they would be stashed in a depot to support his subsequent
longer trip. In the meantime, Amundsen would return to his ship for
the rest of the equipment and food for the trip.

Two men were chosen by *Gjøa's* captain to accompany him. The
threesome left on the first stage of the expedition on March 1, 1904,
with a temperature of –53° C (–63.5° F) on the morning of departure.
Three days on the trail with night temperatures as low as –61° C (–79° F)
soon convinced Amundsen that he had made a mistake in leaving so
early in the season. The third morning, the men decided the temperatures were too severe to continue. They left some supplies and a sled
inside their igloo as a temporary depot, closed it up, marked it with a
flag to find it again, and headed back home to the *Gjøa*. It took them
only four hours to retrace the eleven kilometres (seven miles) they had
struggled over for two-and-a-half days on the trip out in the deep
freeze. Warmer temperatures would have to prevail before Amundsen
set out again. By March 16, that day had arrived.

The 16th dawned as a day with –40 degrees, a temperature that was
much more seasonal and easy to take, although it still sounds mighty
cold to most people. Amundsen chose only one crew member to
accompany him this time, Helmer Hansen. As stated above, the objective for this initial part of their plan to reach Port Leopold was to move
the depot farther north in stages to support the expedition on the final
stage of the eventual trip north. The warmer temperature under a
bright sun made a huge difference in the sliding of their one sled
hitched to ten dogs. Extremely cold temperatures on the first attempt
had made sledding on snow about as slippery as on sand. This time, in
just four hours, they reached their temporary depot where they repos-
sessed the sled left there on the first attempt. The supplies of the depot,
plus what they had with them, were redistributed onto the two sleds,
each carrying 180 kilograms (400 pounds) and pulled by five dogs.

In the morning, after sleeping snugly in the igloo they had built on their previous aborted attempt, the two men set off towards the north. As Amundsen put it, "In the calm weather we went swimmingly over the plains of King William Land. We were soon down in La Trobe Bay, on the east side. We skimmed smoothly over the even ice in the bay and after dusk we erected our tent under a hummock." The tent was a mistake. Fooled by the "warmer" weather, Amundsen decided to forego the relative warmth of a well-built, but time-consuming to construct, igloo. The pair slept in the tent they had brought with them for use in milder weather. That night they "had the bitter experience of the difference between a tent and a snow hut." They spent a night of turning this way and that, knocking their feet together, trying to keep warm. When they got up the next morning, they could not measure the temperature because their thermometer had been broken, but by a rough rule of thumb they deduced that it was at most –50° C (–58° F) The fuel oil they had with them for cooking turned thick and milky white at that temperature, and it was indeed thick and milky white that morning. Getting back on the trail and running alongside the sleds was a real pleasure as the heat of exertion slowly spread through their bodies. The tent was put away. It would be igloos for a while yet.

Amundsen set his course for Matty Island. Opposite the island, across James Ross Strait, was Cape Christian Frederick where he planned to establish the depot to support his later longer trip north. At ten o'clock in the morning, the two Norwegians stopped to tighten the lashings of the sleds, when the eagle eyes of Hansen detected a black dot far out on the ice, which he pronounced to be an Inuk. It was indeed an Arctic aboriginal who was soon joined by several more as they headed towards Amundsen and Hansen. Thirty-four men and boys stopped at a distance of 200 metres (220 yards) and observed the pair without coming any closer. With less trepidation than at his first meeting with the Inuit, Amundsen decided to go to them, with rifle at the ready, just in case. When quite close, he called out "*Manik-tu-mi*" and "it was as if an electric shock had gone through the whole crowd." Thirty-four voices exploded in a chorus of *Manik-tu-mi* and Amundsen trotted right up to the obviously delighted and excited crowd. The Inuit patted and stroked the Norwegians, all the while laughing and shouting their greeting. The exact translation of the magic words is not known, but they were obviously the right words to use when meeting Inuit. These people were called Nechilli Inuit and were of a different tribe than their friends at Gjøahavn, who were called Ogluli Inuit.

Each man carried a spear and had a dog on a leash. They were on foot with their dogs and going to hunt seals, but when Amundsen let it be known that he would like to visit their camp, they were immensely pleased and immediately tied all their dogs to the sleds of the Norwegians. Off went the combined group at a flying clip – there were many dogs now to pull Amundsen's sleds. Great confusion reigned among the excited dogs, with mortal combats breaking out between strangers, requiring expert and sometimes brutal intervention on the part of the Inuit to restore peace. In half an hour, a great cry went up, "Igloo! Igloo!" and sure enough, sixteen domes appeared in the distance.

> The whole place looked quite deserted. We halted a little way off and loosed the dogs. The men made quietly for their huts, and shortly afterwards the fair sex made their appearance. They arranged themselves in single file one behind the other. When all were mustered, the strange procession started running towards us. At the head came old Auva; after her, her friend Anana. 'Running' hardly expresses the movement: they reminded one of a row of waddling geese. They made straight for us, and I trembled; would they kiss us as a sign of welcome? Old Auva was appalling to behold. We had come upon them so abruptly that they had had no time to complete their toilet. Such clothing as Auva had on, was covered with fat and soot, her face shone with train oil [seal oil], and her grayish black hair hung in wild confusion under the hood that had slipped down at the back of her neck. I looked at her with horror as she came nearer.... Nor was Anana beautiful either; she was covered with dirt and soot,

and train oil, but anyone who could survive Auva could easily put up with the other.... I was just expecting the kissing and embracing to commence, when they swerved aside and formed a circle round us, emitting all sorts of weird grunts, and then waddled off back to the camp.... Whether it was pure accident that just the ugliest of them came to us then, or that my taste altered later, I cannot say; certain it is that I afterwards thought some of them were quite good looking.

Now that the greetings were out of the way, Amundsen and Hansen had to put up an igloo for the night. They had no wish to try the tent again before temperatures improved. The Inuit were quite interested in watching the two Norwegians build their snow dwelling, as the latter were of course no experts in the matter. Initial inquisitiveness on the part of the Inuit changed into criticism, which slid into active exultation and finally melted down into uncontrolled laughter. Tears ran down the cheeks of the observers, they writhed with laughter, gasped for breath and positively shrieked. At last the Inuit recovered enough to lend their assistance, taking the whole work in hand, but stopping every now and then as they broke down into laughter at the remembered efforts of the strangers. The end result was that the two Norwegians spent a very comfortable couple of nights in a most beautiful igloo.

The explorers spent the next day visiting Inuit families, trading for clothes and handing out much prized steel needles to the women in return. Amundsen managed to barter for a very fine set of exterior clothes made of caribou skins. Flush with success, he thought he would try for a suit of underclothing as well. His Inuk trading partner, Aitkleura, brought out some old, worn underwear which he himself put on to replace those he was wearing, handing the latter to Amundsen signing that he should put them on right then and there.

Somewhat surprised, I hesitated; I must say I was not in the habit of exchanging underwear with other people, especially in the presence of a lady. But as Aitkleura insisted and his wife, Nalungia, showed the most complete indifference as to what I did, I quickly made my decision, seated myself on the form, veiled my charms as best I could with the bed clothes, and was soon clad in Aitkleura's still warm underclothing.

On the second morning, after a thoroughly enchanting encounter with the Nechilli Inuit, Amundsen and Hansen headed across the ice towards Matty Island accompanied by Poieta, Aitkleura's brother, to help them since he knew the way. At four o'clock that afternoon, just as they stopped for the night, the sky cleared for a moment and revealed Cape Hardy on Matty Island in the distance to the west, and Cape Christian Frederick on Boothia Peninsula to the east. With Poieta's expertise, the igloo went up in record time causing Amundsen to comment on how delightful it was to travel with Inuit, the same comment that my old explorer friend Graham Rowley made more recently in his book *Cold Comfort*.[20]

The next morning was bitterly cold and the fuel was thick and white, meaning at best –50° C (–58° F). At noon the three travellers discovered a small Inuit settlement of six igloos. Poieta absolutely refused to go any farther and returned to his own people. The reason for his abrupt departure may well have had something to do with this new group of Inuit as subsequent events revealed them to not be the best kind of people.

> These Eskimos were on average taller than the Nechilli, and stood about six feet high. But otherwise they produced a much less favourable impression. They had the failing of begging for all they saw. So troublesome did they become that we thought proper to creep into our hut and shut ourselves in. They had of course helped us very kindly in erecting our igloo, but I had no trust in them, and before we went to bed, we lashed our sledge load with extra care; and in this we were right, as the next day we missed a saw, a knife and an axe. After a whole lot of bickering and unpleasantness

we at last succeeded in getting these things back again. But there could be no question of leaving any depot in the neighborhood of these people. The first thing they would do when we were out of sight would obviously be to plunder the whole depot.

The next morning, Amundsen decided to return south to his new-found friends, the Nechelli, in order to leave the depot for his upcoming northern journey in their territory where he felt it would be safe from the depredations of the gang just north of them. As in the case of old workhorses returning to their barn, the return trip went much faster than the trip out; by four o'clock they were back with their good friends the Nechilli.

The Inuit were planning to move south the following day. Amundsen was very interested in seeing the nomadic Inuit on the move, so he and Hansen stayed over in order to participate in their relocation. Meanwhile, he spent the day chatting with the Inuit in their homes, which he very much enjoyed doing. At half past seven the following morning, nine sleds were ready to go, pulled by men, women and dogs.

> Many of the women were employed as draught animals, and smart they were, too, and a pleasure to look at. Not the least pathetic part of it was the good humour with which they tugged away; their faces changed alternately from red to white, and vice versa, from the sharp cold and their own efforts, and I thought many of them quite pretty indeed – this after barely four days' acquaintance with them. They stepped out like men, and in their gait reminded one of young tars, with swinging arms and well bent knees.... They made frequent halts to take breath, and well they might, as their loads were heavy.

As time went on, it is evident that Amundsen began finding Inuit women more and more to his liking. These feelings no doubt started playing havoc with his stated resolve that he and his men should not take liberties with them. As mentioned earlier there is evidence today in Gjoa Haven leading one to conclude that he fell victim to the universal and powerful attraction that exists between men and women. It is fitting, though, that this should happen on an expedition, the purpose of which, was the measurement of the strength of magnetic attraction in the region.

At noon, a halt was called for the day at a place where the Inuit had deposited two sled-loads of meat the previous day. Amundsen tried to convince them to go on with him and Hansen to the ship, but they had plans to spend another day hunting seals, so the Norwegians decided to join them. Twenty Inuit left in a bitterly cold snowstorm with the two *kabluna* (white men) tagging along. As the group spread out, Amundsen paired off with a young Inuk named Anguju to explore inland, neither being interested in the hunting. At the end of the hunt, everyone returned to camp with a total catch of two seals.

The following morning, March 25, the Inuit nomads and the Norwegians continued their trip south in the general direction of the *Gjøa*. At this point Amundsen hid his depot of food a short distance inland where he felt it would not be accessible to the predatory Inuit farther north and asked his friendly Nechilli Inuit to look after it in his absence. He and Hansen parted from the Inuit and continued towards Gjøahavn, travelling the rest of the day and all night, arriving on board the *Gjøa* at eight o'clock on the morning of the 26th of March. At noon there was some excitement as Lieutenant Hansen and Ristvedt, who had been exploring in the absence of Amundsen and Helmer Hansen, arrived back at the ship together, surprisingly, with the thirty-odd Nechilli nomads, whom they had met out on the ice. The Inuit quickly built a small village of igloos not far from the ship, an indication that they were settling in for a while.

Eleven days later, on April 6, Amundsen finally set out on his longer northern trip, accompanied this time by Ristvedt instead of Hansen because Hansen had certain duties on board ship at that time. Amundsen wisely decided to cut short his original plan to go all the way to Port Leopold on the tip of Somerset Island. The youth of his dogs was his stated reason, but it would have been a tough slog for the men, too. He would just have to forego the cache of food and equipment that a Dutch whaler was supposed to have deposited in Port Leopold for him. Although Amundsen never saw it, we now know that the cache was indeed there because A.P. Low, in 1904 on his tour of claiming Arctic Islands for Canada, visited Port Leopold and reported on its presence.

Leaving Gjøahavn, the two Norwegians headed north for the cache they had left in the territory of the Nechilli Inuit at Mount Matheson. They approached it with some apprehension because of the threat of the untrustworthy Inuit some distance farther north, but found that all was in order. Camp was set up using the tent since the temperatures now seldom went lower than −30° C (−22° F). The next morning the two men headed farther north towards Matty Island, now with 270 kilograms (600 pounds) on each sled. The weight was a bit much for the young dogs so the pace was slow. On the evening of April 9, the expedition reached Cape Hardy on Matty Island where Amundsen wanted to set up his first magnetic station. The following morning, Amundsen built the observatory for taking magnetic readings, actually just a curved snow wall to shelter the instruments and the observer from the icy Arctic wind. The observatory was located some two hundred metres from the tent to get it away from the effects of iron objects, but this caused a small problem which Amundsen solved in an imaginative way. The time of taking the observations had to be recorded, but it was very difficult for one man to note the time as well as the observations themselves, not only because of the Arctic temperatures, but also because many of the observations had to be taken at night. A cord was stretched the distance between the observatory and the tent, where it was tied to Ristvedt's arm as he rested comfortably in his sleeping bag. As Amundsen noted each reading, he pulled on the cord, which signalled to Ristvedt that he should record the time.

By April 14, the two men had finished taking magnetic readings. The following morning they mushed on northward. During the day a thick fog enveloped the expedition and, when it stopped for the night, two Inuit materialized out of the gloom. The Inuit were from the same group that had pillaged Amundsen and Hansen's sled loads as they slept earlier in March. Because of the fog and a brewing storm, Amundsen felt that, "...under present circumstances, we had to be on friendly terms with the two gentleman – Kaumallo and Kalakchie. They found their way easily through the dense fog and we were soon at their camp.... They had evidently repented of their previous behaviour and were now very courteous."

The following day a storm and heavy snow blew out of the north making it impossible to continue north with heavily loaded sleds. Amundsen took advantage of the situation by sending Ristvedt and Kalakchie with a lightly loaded sled pulled by all ten of their dogs back to the *Gjøa*, a round trip distance of about 175 kilometres (108 miles), to either repair or replace their one watch, which had been damaged. The capability to know the time is essential for taking magnetic readings. On the evening of April 20, Ristvedt returned and the next morning the men continued on their way. The ice conditions off Matty Island were so bad that to proceed they left one of their sleds on the island. Then, with all ten dogs hitched to the other sled, they crossed James Ross Strait to a point a little north of Cape Christian Frederick. At this point, they stashed the sled load in a depot for future use and returned on foot with all ten dogs to where they had left their first sled at Matty Island, spending the night there at an Inuit camp of three igloos. In his book, Amundsen remarks, "It was among those Eskimo that we saw for the first time little Magito, who afterwards became the belle of Ogchoktu [Gjøahavn]. She was twenty years old, married and very handsome; I was not the only one who thought so." One wonders what role Magito may have played in Amundsen's exploration of Inuit customs.

The two Norwegians pushed on farther north to a point some 175 kilometres (110 miles) southwest of Bellot Strait, which separates Somerset Island from Boothia Peninsula. It was at this point on the mainland of Boothia Peninsula, opposite the Tasmania Islands, that Amundsen established his most northerly magnetic station. He and Ristvedt spent a few days recording their usual set of readings and on May seventh, turned south heading back toward their cache near Cape Christian Frederick. Amundsen's plan was to pick up the supplies in the cache and head some 170 kilometres (105 miles) northeast across

Magito, a young Netsilik-inuit, whom Amundsen found "very handsome." He named her the "belle of Ogchoktu [Gjøahavn]." It is likely that Amundsen met her in 1904. *Courtesy of the National Library of Norway (Portrait of a young Netsilik-inuit, Magito) Picture Collection 1229.*

Boothia Peninsula to Victoria Harbour on its eastern coast. Victoria Harbour had special significance for Arctic explorer Amundsen because it was there that John Ross's ship was abandoned after failing to escape from the deadly embrace of the Arctic ice.

The Arctic journey of Captain John Ross and his second-in-command, nephew James Clark Ross, aboard the *Victory* from 1829 to 1883 was truly remarkable; not just for being the first to send men across Boothia Peninsula to locate the north magnetic pole, but particularly for the saga of endurance and near-death lived by these men when they had to abandon their icebound ship. John Ross's orders directed him to search for the Northwest Passage by going south down Prince Regent Inlet and into the Gulf of Boothia as far as he could to explore the possibilities of that route. By late September, the *Victory* met with very difficult ice conditions that forced her commander to search for a suitable harbour to pass the winter. On October 1, 1829, an excellent wintering port was found, which John Ross named Felix Harbour, after distiller Felix Booth from whom Boothia Peninsula also takes its name. Communications with local Inuit, coupled with the results of surveying and mapping, convinced John Ross that the Northwest Passage would not be found by pushing farther south, so he resolved to retrace his steps and head north when the ice permitted the following summer. However, the low 1830 summer temperatures did not weaken the ice enough to permit *Victory* to escape her icy fetters other than to sail about eight kilometres (five miles) north into her second wintering quarters which John Ross named Sherrif's Harbour. It was while the *Victory* was frozen in at Sherrif's Harbour that nephew James Clark Ross crossed Boothia Peninsula from east to west to home in on the north magnetic pole, arriving at its location on Cape Adelaide Regina on May 1, 1831 . However, the summer of 1831, was no better than the previous one, and that year the *Victory* was only able to move northward a mere 23 kilometres (14 miles) to a new wintering harbour which John Ross named Victory Harbour. (The name was subsequently changed to Victoria Harbour.)

John Ross and his men were now in deep trouble. Their supply of food would last only another eight months or so until June 1832 before starvation or scurvy, or both would set in. They abandoned all hope of trying to save the *Victory* and from then on concentrated on saving their own skins. In the spring of 1932, they began transferring, on foot, whatever provisions they had left north to Fury Point, a distance of some 322 kilometres (200 miles). They finally finished the job and settled there temporarily on July 1, 1832.

Fury Point was named after William Edward Parry's ship the *Fury*, which had come to grief near the point in 1825. But before she sank, her crew had been able to ferry ashore a large quantity of provisions, a good part of which was still there. The ship's crew was rescued by the *Hecla*, the second of Parry's ships on that expedition and made it back to England to sail another day. *Fury*'s cache of food and supplies at Fury Point was a veritable lifesaver for Ross and his men. Here was food enough to prolong their lives many months until, it was hoped, they would be rescued somehow. There was no other alternative. Using materials found in the cache, they built a rudimentary hut in which to pass the winter.

Three of *Fury*'s boats had been left on shore as well. John Ross developed a plan to sail the boats some 170 kilometres north to Lancaster Sound to try and encounter some whaling ships there, which, they hoped, would prove to be their salvation. Ross and his men reached Lancaster Sound that summer, but the sound was completely clogged with ice that year and there were no whalers to be seen. The situation was critical. Their food was beginning to run low, and to stay where they were was certain death. The only alternative was to return to Fury Point and spend a second winter where there were at least a hut and ample supplies left from the *Fury* wreck.

Because of the ice, the men could not sail all the way back to Fury Point. They had to abandon their boats at Batty Point and continue from there on foot, arriving back at the hut and the cache of supplies at Fury Point on October 7, 1832. The following summer, 1833, those who were still able, carried provisions as well as three invalidated men 100 kilometres to the boats abandoned at Batty Bay, and once more John Ross and crew set out for Lancaster Sound in the *Fury*'s boats, providentially finding it clear of ice that year. John and James Ross and the crew of the *Victory* were finally picked up by the *Isabella* of Hull, England, a ship that John Ross himself had once commanded. They were taken back across the Atlantic to their homes after an absence of some four-and-a-half years. In that period of time, there had been only three deaths among the crew of the *Victory*.

Amundsen and Ristvedt headed south toward their depot of food and supplies to pick it up and turn east toward Victoria Harbour to record "A series of magnetic observations here [that] would be very interesting, possibly even more interesting than at the pole itself." However, Amundsen was knocked out of commission by a sore and useless left ankle that he blamed on having laced his boots too tightly. On the 18th of May, after six days as an invalid, he and Ristvedt were finally able to continue toward the depot, only to find that it had been "entirely plundered by our friends Kaumallo and Kalakchie." That effectively put the kibosh on their plans to reach Victoria Harbour. The two men had no choice but to head back to Gjøahavn before they completely ran out of food. They were back on board the *Gjøa* on May 27. Amundsen summed up his trip:

> not a brilliant success; but considering the many untoward circumstances which had occurred, we had to be satisfied with the results.

For the next 14 months, from June 1904 until August 1905, when the expedition sailed away from Gjøahavn to continue its transit of the Northwest Passage, Amundsen and his men occupied themselves with magnetic observations on the one hand, and surveying and mapping on the other. All the while, they lived with, studied and coped with an ever-increasing number of Inuit. Amundsen was very scrupulous about his magnetic data, repeating a number of his previous observations when he suspected some inaccuracies might have crept in. Generally, he found that he was worrying for nothing, but at least his mind was at ease.

On July 18, 1904, upon returning from one of his short trips away for taking magnetic observations, Amundsen learned of a very tragic event that had taken place in his absence on the previous day. An Inuk named Umiktuallu lived with his wife, three children and a foster son. He had an old muzzle-loading rifle, which he was accustomed to leave loaded in his tent when he was not using it. The evening before Amundsen returned, Umiktuallu and his wife were visiting another tent when his foster son and his own eldest son were fooling around with the gun. It went off accidentally and Umiktuallu's son, who was only seven years old, fell to the ground, dead. The father, hearing the shot, rushed to the tent and found his son lifeless on the ground. His foster son was still holding the smoking gun. Crazed with grief and anguish, he grabbed his foster son, dragged him out of the tent and cruelly stabbed him three times through the heart, then kicked him away. Gustav Wiik was a witness to the grisly scene from a certain distance away. Both boys were buried that night. When Amundsen arrived back on board the *Gjøa* that evening, Umiktuallu and his family had already moved away to the mainland.

CHAPTER SIX

The Gjøa's Second Winter, 1904–05

MEMBERS OF TEN DISTINCT TRIBES CAME FROM far and near, attracted by rumours of marvellous happenings at Gjøahavn, or Ogchoktu as they called it. With the exception of one member of the *Gjøa*'s crew, the Norwegians and the Inuit evolved a common language, which was a mixture of Norwegian and Inuktitut words that permitted effective conversation between the two sides to a surprising degree. One is tempted to call it "Norstitut." Amundsen points out that it was clearly not Inuktitut they were speaking. When meeting a previously unknown tribe, neither the Norwegians nor the Inuit could understand a word of what the other was saying at first. It was only with time that they became capable of communicating using the artificial common language.

So many Inuit were semi-permanently gathered in igloos around the *Gjøa* that Amundsen began fearing that should their neighbours for some unfathomable reason – they were after all guided by a number of seemingly illogical taboos – take it into their minds to harm the seven Norwegians, there was really not much they could do about it. The only protection the members of the expedition had was the almost godlike reverence in which the Inuit held them. The more the Inuit and white men became familiar with each other, the more that reverence might decrease in magical power. Amundsen felt it advisable to enhance their image. There was an empty igloo some distance from the ship. Without attracting any undue attention he had a pair of wires, hidden by a covering of snow, run from the igloo to the *Gjøa*. An impressive amount of explosive was placed in the igloo and connected to the wires. At the other end, on board ship, he attached the wires to a hand-operated detonator. It was time for a lesson.

> When that was ready, we collected the Eskimo together on board. I spoke to them about white man's power; that we could spread destruction around us, and even at a great distance accomplish the most extraordinary things. It was, consequently, for them to behave themselves properly and not to expose themselves to our terrible anger. If they should play any tricks on land, for example, over there by the snow huts, then we should merely sit quietly on board and do so.... With a terrific report the igloo blew up, and clouds of snow burst high into the air. This was all that was required.

On Sunday, November 20, 1904, there appeared out of nowhere an unusual Inuk with his family. His first words were "Give me 'moke!" He had obviously had contact with white men. A pipe and tobacco were laid out before him, which he took up, filled the bowl of the pipe with tobacco and lit up. He sat there smoking like a gentleman in a salon and introduced himself: "I am Mr. Atangala." Astounded, Amundsen sat there saying nothing, but was quickly brought to his senses when he was asked, "Might I ask sir, what is your name?"

Atangala, it turned out was a man who had been to Winnipeg with an American whaler and had seen civilization – the telephone, railways, electric lights and whisky. Recently, he and his family had accompanied three white men from his home of Chesterfield Inlet in Hudson Bay to the Coppermine River and he was on his way back home when he decided to take a 320 kilometre (200 miles) detour to Ogchoktu. He had heard that there was a vessel with which he might be able to do business. He came with very interesting news for the Norwegians – two large vessels were overwintering at Fullerton Harbour near Chesterfield Inlet. Amundsen saw this as a great opportunity to send news back home to Norway via these ships. He immediately hired Atangala as a courier, commissioning him to take a packet of mail to Fullerton Harbour by dogsled, a mere 580 kilometres (360 miles) one way as the crow flies!

Everyone on board ship started furiously writing letters home, welcoming the opportunity to advise family and friends of their successes and good health. There was now also the possibility of receiving news from the outside world from these as yet unknown ships when, and if, Atangala came back. For all the Norwegians knew, Mr. Atangala might be the world's biggest fraud; only time would tell, a considerably long period of time, many months in fact. On November 28, Mr. Atangala set out with his precious bundle of mail at eleven o'clock in the morning, literally disappearing into the Arctic mists.

Christmas soon descended upon the tiny *Gjøa* and her seven voluntary exiles in the dark of the Arctic winter. Each of the crewmembers no doubt had his own private fond and longing thoughts about his loved ones back home. That year, the parcels marked "Do not open before 1904" were eagerly opened and enjoyed. As before, one of the most important men of the *Gjøa* crew at all times, but particularly at Christmastime, was the cook, Adolf Henrik Lindstrøm. He was once more an extremely busy man labouring down in the hold of the ship where his kitchen was set up during the winter. Roasts, stews, pies, biscuits, cakes, loaves of bread – all manner of food had to be prepared in advance to satisfy the healthy appetites of the crew.

Lindstrøm was the four-star *cordon bleu* of the Arctic and later of the Antarctic as well. People stationed or travelling in the polar regions for extended periods of time in those days were necessarily deprived of many of the pleasures of normal life. They would suffer most of these

Adolf Lindstrøm, the cook, on King William Island in the autumn of 1904 with raw material for his meals. *From* The North West Passage *by Roald Amundsen.*

lacks with relative equanimity, but there was one item the absence of which they absolutely would not tolerate – excellent food and lots of it. One of Captain Otto Sverdrup's biggest worries during his fourth, unexpected overwintering of the *Fram* off the coast of Ellesmere Island in 1901–02 was that the ship's larder was running low of certain luxuries: "As for our provisions, what I feared most was that we might run short of butter and coffee. Our after-dinner coffee was struck off the menu and the butter scales were put into use."

Lindstrøm's cooking was all Amundsen and his men could have desired. Being no lightweight himself, the cook knew that quantity as well as quality was essential. Variety was not missing from the menu either. Polar bear, caribou, walrus, seal, goose, ptarmigan and other game birds graced the *Gjøa's* table in various forms. Fresh bread was baked daily and four or five pancakes per man were the order of the day for breakfast – every day. This was not Lindstrøm's first experience as Polar cook nor his last. He had been an essential member of the crews of the first and second *Fram* expeditions and he was to keep stomachs happy on Amundsen's trip to the South Pole from 1910 to 1912. Scurvy never raised its ugly head on any of Lindstrøm's watches, due undoubtedly to the variety of properly cooked fresh meats available to the crews on all his trips.

Lindstrøm was more than just a good cook; he became the expedition's best practitioner of bartering. The cook's bartering skills were honed early on in the trip while the *Gjøa* was still off the coast of Greenland though he didn't speak a word of Inuktitut:

> Lindstrøm knew how to make matters go smoothly – in his own way. He was busy everywhere, bought from and bartered with the Eskimo, now a salted salmon, now a fresh one, now an eider duck, now a loon. Lindstrøm's coin was baker Hansen's mouldy spiced cakes from Christiania [Oslo]... When an Eskimo came to sell, Lindstrøm was fetched on deck. The negotiations were carried on in Eskimo and good Nordland Norse... We who knew that our dear cook had not the faintest notion of Eskimo, gathered in couples ready to burst with laughter. When the discussion had lasted some time, Lindstrøm would suddenly show a bright gleam of intelligence and disappear into the hold. Big-looking and benign he would come back again with a mouldy spiced cake under each arm. The Eskimo regarded Lindstrøm with astonishment, as he asked for tobacco in exchange for his salmon. Any attempt to make Lindstrøm understand his error is met with a thorough, condescending, shoulder-shrugging non comprehension. Lindstrøm takes the salmon, the man takes the cakes and the transaction is finished. The epilogue is perhaps, after all the best of it: to hear Lindstrøm relate that he, of course, understood every word uttered by the Eskimo, "but as he asked for three cakes, I pretended I did not understand, and gave him two." I had my dark suspicion that the Eskimo had taken cakes to his own people more than once, and, undoubtedly with better reason, boasted to them that "he [the Inuk] had pretended he did not understand."

Lindstrøm also became the expedition's official collector and pre-
server of botanical and zoological specimens. His own collecting and
that of the men were not the only sources of these specimens. He
enlisted the Inuit to become collectors for him by bartering with items
desirable to them. At times, though, the power of his bartering skills
got out of hand.

> Lindstrøm gave prizes, principally consisting of old
> underwear, for which the Eskimo contested eagerly.
> Later on we met Eskimo on King William Land strut-
> ting about in Lindstrøm's worn-out pantaloons, etc.
> Altogether, he worked indefatigably, and he endeav-
> ored to obtain a specimen of every living creature in
> the region. Even the special kind of *pediculus capitis*
> [head lice, a delicious snack enjoyed by the Inuit],
> which the Eskimo rejoiced in had to be obtained, and
> Lindstrøm offered prizes for specimens. At first very
> few specimens were obtainable, but when the Eskimo
> understood that it was really a business matter, they
> came daily in crowds, bringing specimens to Lindstrøm.
> What had previously been Lindstrøm's joy was now his
> despair, and it required all his energy to put an end to
> this business and keep the pediculi at a distance, but
> even then he had enough of all varieties to furnish a
> good supply to every zoological collection in Europe.

The cook also turned out to be quite a marksman with many a
ptarmigan falling victim to his shotgun. Lund and Hansen decided
one morning to appeal to Lindstrøm's love of birding to play a trick on
him. They set up a frozen ptarmigan, killed two months previously, in
a lifelike position on top of a snowdrift some 25 metres (80 feet) in
front of the ship. "Lindstrøm! Lindstrøm!" cried Lund. "There is a
ptarmigan on the ice!" The cook was on deck in a flash with his gun.
"Where is it?" "There, on the bow." He stealthily aimed at the bird and
let go with a blast from the ship's forward deck. The ptarmigan rolled

over on the ice. "Ha! Ha! I hit him that time" cried the nimrod as he leapt over the side and ran to fetch his bird. For a time he stood with the bird in his hand feeling it all over. "Why, it is quite cold," he observed in a somewhat confused and disappointed tone. The peals of laughter from the ship, however, soon let him in on the fact that he had been duped once more.

Lindstrøm was a happy-go-lucky, somewhat gullible, type who was often the butt of such practical jokes played on him. His endearing quality, though, was that each time he realized he had been caught yet again, he was the one who laughed the loudest. He was quite a popular member of his crew and supplied the expedition with a bit of much-needed levity to lighten the demanding and very serious business of Arctic exploration.

Although the white men appeared extremely powerful to the Inuit, there was one thing more powerful still – the Inuit taboos. Even though they were short of food, the Inuit did not go seal hunting in the new year until the middle of January.

> As far as I could see, the moon had to have a certain position before they dared go seal catching.... A great number of the women folk had constant sewing work from us for which we made some slight payment, much to their satisfaction; but one fine day they all declared that they could not work. We questioned them and learnt that the first seal had been caught, and that the women had eaten its flesh; it was consequently impossible for them to do any work other than their own until the sun was at a certain height in the sky. We explained to them the stupidity of the whole thing; we promised them higher wages, indeed almost begged and entreated them to continue their work for us, but all in vain; they were proof against ordinary human arguments. Here God or the Devil stood behind and the women refused to comply with our request, although otherwise they were very submissive

and always ready to oblige. Old Navya was the only one who had been sensible enough to abstain from eating seal flesh. She now came on board and sewed for us from morning until evening, the object of all our admiration.

During the coldest days of the winter even the Inuit, who were inured to living in the extreme, bitterly low temperatures of the Arctic, limited their outings to the strictly necessary. Their untaxed bodies must have told them that they needed exercise and diversion to remain healthy and the natural reaction was to respond by exercising and amusing themselves indoors. It's not that there was a logical thinking process at play here, but rather that the Inuit were no doubt responding to a natural urge in a completely instinctual manner; in other words they enjoyed doing what was required to maintain health much as we enjoy skiing, skating, jogging, snowshoeing and other winter sports.

The Inuit answer was to build a large communal igloo where they practised gymnastics, conjuring, singing and dancing. Men of all ages engaged in gymnastics, even the elders acquitted themselves as well as the younger men. Having no wood to make a horizontal bar was not a problem for the ever-ingenious Inuit. They improvised a long cable out of five sealskin straps laid down together with an additional sealskin strap coiled tightly around the five making a very reliable bar when frozen. Holes were made, one on each side of the igloo at the right height. One end of the rope was passed through one of the holes and tied to a wooden bar outside which was secured crosswise to the snow, probably by freezing. Then the other end was threaded through the opposite hole, stretched taut and tied to a second wooden bar which was secured crosswise to the snow in the same fashion as the first. Then the show began.

Using this horizontal bar, the Inuit performed some of the same gymnastic moves that Amundsen himself used to practise in his younger days, much to his amazement. Young and old, the Inuit were supple and agile. Amundsen tried to display his own long-unpractised gymnastics skills but failed miserably, giving the halfhearted excuse that he was not used to a rope of sealskin in place of a horizontal bar.

Amundsen left us some insight into the effects of civilization upon the primitive Inuit:

> Evidently they enjoyed life, but on the other hand, they had not the slightest fear of death. If they were sick or in misery they bade farewell to life with a tranquil mind and strangled themselves. Two such cases occurred during our sojourn among them. During the voyage of the "Gjøa" we came into contact with ten different Eskimo tribes in all, and we had good opportunities of observing the influence of civilisation on them, as we were able to compare those Eskimo who had come into contact with civilisation with those who had not. And I must state as my firm conviction that the latter, the Eskimo living absolutely isolated from civilisation, are undoubtedly the happiest, healthiest, most honourable and most contented among them... My sincerest wish for our friends the Nechilli Eskimo is, that civilisation may never reach them.

On April 2, 1905, Lieutenant Hansen and Peter Ristvedt left Gjøahavn on a major dogsled trip to an unmapped stretch of the east coast of Victoria Island along McClintock Channel in an effort to complete the cartography of that part of the island. Amundsen believed that stretch of coast was "the only portion of the North American Archipelago which has not been mapped." In that belief he was not correct. Stefansson had yet to discover the last five significant islands in the western part of the Archipelago known today as Brock, Borden and Mackenzie King islands, found in 1915, plus Meighen and Lougheed in 1916. As well, a 300-kilometre (180-mile) stretch of Baffin Island coastline along Foxe Basin was mapped for the first time in 1937 by Canadian Arctic explorers Graham Rowley and Reynold Bray, accompanied by two Inuit. Thus was completed the mapping job first undertaken by Martin Frobisher more than 400 years earlier.

Lieutenant Hansen and Ristvedt had food for seventy-five days including that which had been placed in a depot established at Cape Crozier the previous year on the westernmost extremity of King William Island. They set out for Victoria Island in a westerly direction on April 2, 1905, on an expedition into the unknown that lasted more days than they or the five men left behind on the *Gjøa* could have imagined; more than they had food for. It would be some time before their shipmates would see them again.

May 20, 1905, was a red-letter day on board the *Gjøa*. By 9:30 in the evening, Amundsen and his crew had just gone to bed when a man burst into the cabin announcing, "Go' morning! You give me 'moke!" Amundsen knew immediately that it was Atangala, and that could only mean one thing. He had just returned from his postal errand to Fullerton Harbour on which he had set out from Gjøahavn six months previously, carrying, it was hoped, messages from the men aboard the two unknown ships that overwintered there. All five of the crew remaining aboard rushed out to Atangala to get the mail he had brought back with him. As Amundsen and his men waited impatiently in the snow, Atangala dug into the bowels of his sled load and came up with a small soldered tin box from under his pile of odds and ends. That was the mail!

> I shall not endeavour to describe my feelings when holding this tin box in my hands, containing as it did messages from the living tumultuous world. We well knew that there could not be any direct messages from the dear ones at home, but, here, at least, was news of the great human community to which we all belonged, and from which we had so long been cut off. The simple word "mail" produced an indescribable sensation in us all.

The first letter he opened was from Major J.D. Moodie, Superintendent of the Royal North West Mounted Police, who was in command of the 1904–05 expedition of the Canadian ship *Arctic* under the captaincy of master mariner Joseph Elzéar Bernier. The *Arctic* had been sent into Hudson Bay to overwinter there and establish Canadian control of the whaling operations in that region, which were carried out mainly by Americans. In the second year, 1905, the *Arctic* was to proceed into the Arctic Archipelago to reinforce Canadian sovereignty over its northern islands. In addition to this letter, Superintendent Moodie sent a gift of five sled dogs to Amundsen via Atangala.

Captain Bernier also wrote a letter to Amundsen containing valuable information on the American whalers operating on the northwest coast of North America. This information would be useful to the Norwegian captain when the *Gjøa* finally broke out of the narrow confines of the western end of the Northwest Passage into the Beaufort Sea. Bernier also sent many newspaper clippings and photographs "which we greedily devoured."

American whaler Captain Comer of the *Era*, who was also wintering in Fullerton Harbour, sent a warm and friendly letter as well as five more sled dogs. Amundsen had asked for the dogs hoping that they would arrive before the Victoria Island expedition of Lieutenant Hansen and Ristvedt set out, but that did not happen. Amundsen then sent back the ten dogs, which he could no longer use, to the generous Moodie and Comer with lavish thanks and regrets via Atangala on his way back home to Chesterfield Inlet. Atangala must have set some kind of record for distance covered by dogsled in a six or seven month period.

It was the end of May 1905 and time to begin gradually packing up in preparation for continuing west on through the Northwest Passage. The first order of business was to dismantle the stores building which had been built of wooden packing boxes, put the remaining stores in the boxes, and the wooden boxes in their metal cases. These cases were numbered and entered in the stores list to keep track of what was where on board ship. With the help of three Inuit, the stores were sledded to the ship's side, hoisted on board and lowered into the hold. A carefully drawn up plan of the stowage was made so that anything could be found at any time.

The Norwegians had made up eleven piles of wood and metal for which they had no more use and rewarded those Inuit who had worked assiduously for them over the months with a pile each. To those thus rewarded, these piles represented untold riches and each was proud to bursting with his treasure trove of wood and metal. There were also hundreds of empty tins left over, which were useless to the Norwegians but veritable jewels to the Inuit. Amundsen gathered together all the Inuit women around the pile of tins each with her man behind her and organized a competition. At the count of three, the women were to rush to the pile and start tossing tins between their legs back to their husbands for them to catch. Such an event, tremendously hilarious to all, was hard to beat, accompanied as it was with laughter and noise, shrieks and shouts, tins flying, men rushing, and so the heap was cleared.

In the beginning of June, the self-registering instruments for recording magnetic data were dismantled and carefully packed away after nineteen months of trouble-free service. It was now the 16th of June and the Victoria Island expedition of Lieutenant Hansen and Ristvedt should have been back by then, but there was no sign of the two men – they had left 84 days previously. Amundsen began to worry. On June 24, 1905, St. John the Baptist day, at 6:30 in the morning, Lund, who had the watch, woke Amundsen, announcing, "Here are the boys."

> I was not long dressing. It was a splendid morning, perfectly calm, with a burning hot sun, and there were our two comrades approaching... I can hardly say how glad and relieved I was to see them and the rate at which they drove the dogs went a long way to show that the animals were still in good condition.

Lieutenant Hansen and Ristvedt had been on the trail 84 days although they had left with food for only 75 days, including a cache of 20 days' food that had been made the year before some 13 days from Gjøahavn. When the cache was reached, it was found that bears had completely destroyed it, so theoretically that reduced their food supply to enough only for a total round trip of 55 days. But they had been gone 84 days. Hunting had been so good – caribou, seals, bears, ptarmigan

– that lack of food had never been an issue. On May 26, 1905, Lieutenant Hansen and Ristvedt decided that it was time to go back. What made them turn around was the advancing season. It wouldn't do for bad weather and open water to prevent them from getting back to the *Gjøa* in time for the ship's departure. It was disappointing to them that they were leaving 161 kilometres (100 miles) of the coast still unmapped, but discretion being the better part of valour, they headed home, making it back to Gjøahavn in a month less two days.

At three o'clock in the morning, August 13, 1905, the seven Norwegians sailed their ship out of Gjøahavn forever and into Simpson Strait, turning her prow southwest into the same doubtful navigational conditions that had kept them so much on the alert when they had been heading south down Rae Strait two years before, just prior to finding their cozy harbour – impenetrable fog, no compass and a very changeable breeze. Sounding with the lead was essential. Some 15 hours or so after leaving Gjøahavn, a cairn of heaped up stones on shore was passed by in silence and with colours flying as a mark of honour. The previous year, Lieutenant Hansen and Helmer Hansen had found two skeletons of Franklin's men, identified by their accoutrements, at this point and had buried them with due respect. For the next 14 days, Amundsen and his men grappled with the most dangerous, intricate and nerve-wracking navigation of the trip as they threaded their way through the little known waters of Queen Maud Gulf, Dease Strait, Coronation Gulf and finally into Dolphin and Union Strait. Their path was studded with a peppering of small islands, shoals and ice. Fog caused them to throw out the anchor behind protective islands for hours at a time to wait out the mists. Even when there was no fog, there were many times that stopping and anchoring was necessary to take position observations, verifying precisely where they were before continuing on for even short distances. The danger and tension took its toll on the captain.

> I cannot deny that I had felt very nervous the last few days. The thought that here in these troublesome waters we were running the risk of spoiling the whole

of our so far successful enterprise was anything but pleasant, but it was always present to my mind. The whole responsibility for crew and the vessel rested on me, and I could not get rid of the possibility of return- ing home with the task unperformed. The thought was anything but cheering. My hours of rest and sleep were principally spent, during this time, in brooding over such thoughts, and they were not very conducive to sleep. All our precautions and everybody's careful attention not withstanding, any moment might have some surprise in store for us. I could not eat. At every mealtime I felt a devouring hunger, but I was unable to swallow my food. When finally we got out of our scrapes and I regained our usual calm, I had a most rapacious hunger to satisfy, and I would rather not mention what I managed to dispose of.

Once the *Gjøa* was well ensconced in Dolphin and Union Strait, Amundsen knew that the most critical part of navigating the Northwest Passage was behind him. His ship was now in waters that had been furrowed before by the hulls of ships coming from the west. That is not to say there wouldn't still be many challenges before him, but they would generally be of a different sort and of a somewhat less critical nature with respect to threatening the success of his venture.

The Northwest Passage is a waterway between the Atlantic and Pacific oceans. The *Gjøa* was still many kilometres from Pacific waters, which can be said to start south of the Aleutian Islands – some 4,000 kilometres (2,500 miles) away. A lot can happen to a 47-ton wooden sailing vessel in 4,000 kilometres, especially when sailing the Beaufort Sea, Bering Strait and the Gulf of Alaska.

At eight o'clock in the morning on August 27, 1905, Amundsen, had retired to his bed after his watch topside. He had been asleep for some time, when a commotion on deck dragged him roughly out of his slumber. Lieutenant Hansen rushed into his cabin crying. "Vessel in sight, sir!" Amundsen was dressed and on deck in a flash. Everyone

The *Gjøa* encountering its first set of American whalers. *From* The North West Passage *by Roald Amundsen.*

else was already on deck, smiling, peering through binoculars and telescopes at the ship, still in the distance, which was to bring them their first, face-to-face, human contact with people from the outside world in over two years. Was it an American ship, an English ship? As the vessels closed, the Norwegian flag was proudly hoisted on high to the top of the *Gjøa*'s mast. The Norwegians squinted across the waves at the stranger waiting for her to show her colours. "She's an American!," shouted the Norwegians as the stars-and-stripes were hoisted aloft.

The Norwegians scurried around to tidy up their vessel and then went below to change into their best clothes. Four were to go aboard the American, the other three staying on board to take care of the *Gjøa*. The crew lowered a dory and Amundsen with three sailors rowed across the tossing waves to be welcomed on board the *Charles Hanson* by Captain James McKenna. He was jovial and agreeable, asking if there was anything the Norwegians wanted, that he could provide. *News* is what the men wanted, news from home, but that he could not provide. The only thing he could offer them was old newspapers. They may have been old to him, but to the Norwegians, they were absolutely fresh. A headline caught their attention – "War between Norway and Sweden." Nineteen hundred and five is the year Norway became free of the Swedish Crown. This was news indeed, though somewhat worrisome news almost devoid of details. The Norwegians spent two hours on board, Amundsen getting invaluable information from Captain McKenna about ice conditions on his proposed route forward and how best to cope with them. It looked like there were good possibilities of sailing in open leads all the way to Herschel Island off the coast of the Yukon, close to the border with Alaska, and from there on to San Francisco to complete their voyage that year, 1905. Herschel Island was an important station for American whalers. There would be many experienced seamen there from whom Amundsen could to get invaluable, up to date advice on how to proceed along the ice-ridden, treacherous northern coast of mainland Canada.

Amundsen was itching to continue on his way to catch the fair breeze that blew, so with gracious thanks, he took leave of Captain McKenna and rowed back to the *Gjøa*, thoroughly pleased that he had made his first contact with civilization after coming though all the previously unsailed stretches of the Northwest Passage. There was no time to lose if they were to get out of the Arctic in 1905. Alas, it was not to be. Ice conditions along the northern coast of mainland Canada that year did not even allow the *Gjøa* to reach Herschel Island, let alone escape the Arctic. Although Amundsen did not know it yet, King Point, some 60 kilometres (36 miles) east of Herschel Island, was to be the home of the *Gjøa* for the next ten months.

CHAPTER SEVEN

The Gjøa's Third Winter, 1905–06

THERE WAS NOTHING MUCH AT KING POINT other than a wrecked schooner, the *Bonanza*, her second mate, Norwegian Christian Sten, a few crew and some Inuit, but at least it was company. Amundsen and his men started knocking together a home ashore for the winter, as Christian Sten was also doing for himself. Amundsen, Lieutenant Hansen and a young Inuit man, Manni, who had been taken on board as the ship left Gjøahavn, would live on board the ship to take care of it and the five other crew members would move into the house being built by them. By September 7, 1905 the sea ice was strong enough to walk on. *Gjøa*'s third winter in the Arctic had started. As they had done at Gjøahavn, Amundsen and Wiik set up the instruments for making magnetic observations. Their ice-enforced time at King Point would not be wasted.

One thing was not lost on Amundsen: the fact that at King Point, he was close to telegraphic communication with the outside world. Closeness is only relative. Telegraph wires from southern civilization

Manni, a young Inuit from Gjøahavn. Amundsen was taking him back to Norway to receive an education. *From* The North West Passage *by Roald Amundsen.*

stretched as far north as Eagle City, Alaska, some 800 kilometres (500 miles) by dogsled south of Herschel Island through the Alaskan and Yukon wilderness. Amundsen thought he was only about 483 kilometres (300 miles) from a telegraph station, which he thought to be at Fort Yukon, when in reality he was closer to the 800 kilometres away. Eagle City was an Alaskan frontier outpost on the Yukon River established in 1897, during the Klondike Gold Rush, less than ten kilometres (six miles) from the Alaska-Yukon Boundary. There was an operating telegraph line in 1905 and Amundsen planned to use it to get news from home and to let his family, the families of his crew, Norway and the whole world, know that the *Gjøa* was on the verge of completing the first ever marine transit of the famed Northwest Passage and that the following year, 1906, would see him achieve his objective.

On October 21 at six o'clock in the morning, Amundsen left King Point by dogsled with Manni, heading for Herschel Island on the first leg of the journey to Eagle City to let the world know where he was. On the trail, by pure chance, he met an Inuk, Jimmy, who was going to carry Herschel Island mail destined for the outside world to Fort Yukon, which was on the way to Eagle City. Amundsen was pleased to meet Jimmy and was impressed by him. He and Jimmy made plans to travel together at least as far as Fort Yukon which was a fair bit more than half way to Eagle City. Arriving at Herschel Island that after- noon, Manni complained of pains in his legs and asked to be left behind. Amundsen agreed rather than trying to convince him to go on against his will. The Norwegian made arrangements with a Captain Mogg to travel with him. Mogg had been the master of the *Bonanza* before she was wrecked at King Point. There would be two dog teams – Amundsen and Mogg with one sled pulled by five dogs, plus Jimmy and his wife Kappa with the other sled pulled by seven dogs. Much as in the case of a two-ship expedition, Mogg was com- mander of the overall expedition, whereas Amundsen and Jimmy were each "captain" of his own respective team. Although the expedi- tion was not carrying enough dog food for the whole trip, it was expected that they would meet up with Inuit, and later with Indians, when they entered forested country, from whom they could buy meat and fish for their dogs and themselves.

Food for humans carried by the expedition consisted of pork and beans already cooked, frozen and packed in meal-sized portions, plus wheat biscuits, rice, sugar, butter, tea, coffee, chocolate, milk, figs, raisins and spices. Amundsen remarked that, "It was certainly a much richer list of stores than I was accustomed to, but I had my doubts as to whether in solidity this variety would compare with the simpler stores used for our sledge trips.... We also took with us a tent and tent poles, stove, lamp, sleeping bags, and many other luxuries." It is interesting to note what Amundsen considered luxuries. These stores would be augmented by meat and fish bartered along the way. When the expedi- tion reached the forest with its deep, soft snow, their Inuit sleds would no longer be appropriate; therefore, each team carried an Indian toboggan on top of their loads.

At nine o'clock in the morning on October 24, the expedition departed Herschel Island with the mail packet destined for Fort Yukon, from where the letters and packages would be forwarded to the outside world. Amundsen and Mogg would then carry on, first to Circle City, and then to Eagle City to reach the telegraph office, leaving Jimmy and Kappa at Fort Yukon.

An Inuit family in the summer with their skin tent in the background. *From* The North West Passage *by Roald Amundsen.*

On the evening of the 26th of October, the expedition encountered its first trees, which quite excited Amundsen since he had not seen any trees after leaving Norway some two years before. Amundsen wrote that on the morning of the following day,

> ...the landscape suddenly appeared like a piece of gen-
> uine Norwegian scenery, timbered and rocky. The little
> valley was closely covered with trees, and from the
> lowest point there rose a huge snow cone to a height of
> quite 2,000 feet, while in the bosom of the valley nes-
> tled two little tents, like pictures from a fairy scene,
> with the smoke rising peacefully from the chimneys.

The occupants of the tents were two Inuit men and their wives. The men were away hunting caribou and mountain goats. Amundsen, Mogg, Jimmy and Kappa set up their communal tent and camped with the two Inuit couples for the rest of the day and night. They bartered with them for meat which was a welcome change from pork and beans. The following day the expedition pushed on and soon met more Inuit who had killed fourteen caribou and so they had another bellyful, as well as bartering tea for even more meat to load onto their sleds.

By then, the snow conditions had changed enough to make their Inuit sleds useless, so they switched to their Indian toboggans. The sleds were leaned up against trees to be picked up again on the return trip. According to their map, the expedition crossed the border from Canada into Alaska at this point. Needless to say, there were no border formalities. Jimmy's knowledge of the route ended here, but with their map, the expedition team was able to carry on.

Amundsen was quite proud of his Norwegian skis, but at times he regretted not having brought snowshoes like the others. For travelling through a forested area on a non-maintained trail, snowshoes are much more efficient than skis, as the skis are always getting hung up in the bushes, trees and other vegetation. The expedition tobogganed on, meeting more and Native People as they approached Fort Yukon at the confluence of the Yukon and Porcupine rivers, which they reached in the afternoon of November 20. This was the end of the line for Jimmy and Kappa, she being quite worn out by this time and very glad to rest. Jimmy delivered his mail packet to the postal authority in Fort Yukon for onward transmittal to more southern locations.

Amundsen was quite disappointed with Fort Yukon because he thought the telegraph station was there when in fact it was some 320 kilometres (200 miles) farther south in Eagle City. He hired an Indian guide, Charlie, to accompany himself and Mogg as they did not know the way. Charlie would take them as far as Circle City which was roughly 110 kilometres farther on where other arrangements would have to be made to continue the last 218 kilometres (135 miles) to Eagle City. It took the men until the 26th of November to reach Circle City, sleeping at times in huts or cabins along the way. Amundsen was quite glad to be rid of Charlie, whom he found to be arrogant and disagreeable.

To his great joy, Amundsen discovered that a mail carrier, Mr. Harper, would be setting out southward for Eagle City the next morning. The news could not have been better. The three men would travel together with two toboggans. This last stretch was somewhat more civilized with a system of so-called road houses – small log huts providing food and lodging for travellers. These were situated along the Yukon River at intervals of about thirty-two kilometres (twenty miles) and generally consisted of three rooms – one for the guests, one for the kitchen and one for the owner of the hut. Those who travelled without their own beds had to share with another. This arrangement did not bother people in those parts. They were so dead tired when they arrived at the log huts that they would probably have slept comfortably on beds of nails.

In early December, Amundsen and Mogg finally reached Eagle City:

> I now approached Eagle City with great excitement. At last I was to be in direct communication with home, and get all the news from my own fatherland. As we rounded the last point, there, only two miles away, lay Eagle City with its blue smoke standing out darkly against the bright sky. You can imagine how overpowering is the thought that within a few hours you will be in touch with the dear ones at home. When we got near the town, we left the ice and drove into the city to the telegraph office... I dispatched my precious telegram, which was only just in time, as shortly afterwards the wires broke, owing to the intense cold.

Amundsen spent the next two months in Eagle City awaiting answers from Norway to his telegraphed messages as well as the southern mail bound for Herschel Island. On February 3, 1906, Amundsen set out on his return trip. As detailed as the description of his outward leg is, as succinct is the account of his return journey.

> I then started for the north. The whip cracked, the dogs pulled and we were off northwards – to the "Gjøa" and my comrades.... On March 12th at 6 P.M. I was back on board and brought newspapers and letters for all.

Shortly after Amundsen's return, Gustav Wiik began to feel unwell. On March 26, he was struck with acute pains on his right side. A couple of days later he took to his bed. Amundsen treated him as best he could according to the medical books he had and with the medicines available to him. Wiik's pulse raced between 104 and 116 and his temperature was in the 102° to 104° F range. On April 1, seeing that Wiik's condition was not improving, Amundsen was making arrangements to transport him by dogsled the 60 kilometres to Herschel Island where a doctor lived, when Wiik breathed his last. It is thought that he may have died from a burst appendix.

Wiik's death was quite a shock to the remaining members of the expedition.

> Wiik was everybody's friend. His humour and jocularity had afforded us many happy hours. Death must always be a gruesome guest, but to us, in our position far away from friends and relations, it was if possible, more depressing than it would otherwise have been. As soon as possible we resumed work, the great consoler and helper.

Since, Amundsen's ship would now be short one crew member, Dr. Wight of Herschel Island asked if he could become part of the *Gjøa's* crew for the trip down south as he had had news that one of his family members was ill. Amundsen took him on commenting that "we should be quite full up."

On July 11, 1906, the first whaler from the south was able to get through the ice and reach King Point. Seeing this, Amundsen prepared to leave. He finally gave the command, "Cast off! Full speed ahead!" The *Gjøa* was on the last and final leg of her historic journey. She headed west past Herschel Island and some distance further, but the shifting ice forced her back and the ship had to enter the harbour at Herschel Island to wait things out.

As the ship had sailed out of Gjøahavn at the end of their stay there, Amundsen had taken on board Manni, a young Inuit man whom he wanted to take back to Norway with him to be educated. Manni had turned out to be a willing and useful member of the crew and was a favourite with the men. He was a good hunter of ducks for the *Gjøa's*

A battered *Gjøa* arriving in Nome, Alaska. *From* The North West Passage *by Roald Amundsen.*

larder, a job he enjoyed doing. On July 21, Amundsen and three others set out by rowboat to examine the condition of the ice along the coast that was keeping his ship prisoner. On their way back they came in view of the *Gjøa* and saw a troubling sight – her flag was flying at half mast, which was most unusual. Hurrying back and quickly climbing on board, Amundsen was told by Lieutenant Hansen that Manni had drowned. One minute he had been standing in his boat, shooting at ducks and the next minute his boat was empty, and he had disappeared. Like all Inuit, he had never learned to swim. His body was never found.

> We had all become fond of him and were very anxious
> to take him with us to civilised regions and see what
> we could make of him there.

While waiting at Herschel after a few more false starts, Amundsen wrote that he met "A Mr. Steffensen [sic] who came in with the mail" from the south. This man was Vilhjalmur Stefansson, the Canadian explorer who would later become famous for his discoveries of new islands in the western Canadian Arctic during his Canadian Arctic Expedition of 1913–18.

It was not before the evening of August 10 that Amundsen weighed anchor and could report that, "At 6 p.m. the fog lifted and revealed a

Six happy crew members at Nome. Left to right, standing at back: Godfred Hansen and Anton Lund; front row: Roald Amundsen, Peder Ristvedt, Adolf Lindstrøm and Helmer Hansen. *From* The North West Passage *by Roald Amundsen.*

gladdening sight. We had got into the open channel along the coast and had a clear course to the west as far as we could see."

The next three weeks pitted Amundsen and his men against some of the most dangerous sailing of the whole voyage with the *Gjøa* having to sail a fine line between pack ice to the north, and a shallow bottom along the mainland to the south, complicated by a drive shaft bent by the ice putting the engine out of commission and a broken gaff in the rigging that prevented the mainsail from being hoisted. The *Gjøa* had to sail with the trysail only which meant that she could not tack. Fortunately, she had a tailwind at the time and was able to limp the last kilometres to Nome, Alaska, for repairs. In anchoring off Nome, Amundsen and his men won the well deserved honour of being the first sailors ever to sail a ship through the entire length of the Northwest Passage. The date was August 31, 1906. The people of Nome greeted the men of the expedition with an enthusiastic, lively and noisy American-style party by way of congratulations.

After surviving the Nome celebrations and the rigours of Bering Strait, Amundsen and his crew sailed the *Gjøa* safely through the Gulf of Alaska and the North Pacific to her final anchorage in San Francisco Harbour, mission accomplished. The Norwegian graciously made a gift of the *Gjøa* to the citizens of the California city where she spent several years on display in Golden Gate Park. By November 1906, Amundsen and his crew were back in Norway where they were greeted as returning heroes by tumultuous, cheering crowds. In 1972, the now famous *Gjøa* was repatriated to her rightful home, Norway, where today she rests ashore at Bygdøy in Oslo Harbour next to two other famous Norwegian exploration vessels – Fridtjof Nansen's *Fram* and Thor Heyerdahl's *Kon-Tiki*.

CHAPTER EIGHT

Amundsen, The Sequel

SAILING THE NORTHWEST PASSAGE FROM END
to end was an exploit that shared a characteristic with the exploits of
reaching the North and South poles – none of these exploits held any
significant intrinsic value for mankind. American explorer Admiral
Richard Byrd said of the South Pole, it "lies in the centre of a limitless
plain. And that is almost all that can be said of it. It is the effort of getting there that counts."[21] These exploits were similar in this respect to
running the four-minute mile, climbing Mount Everest, or even, some
would claim, setting foot on the moon. However, they all brought great
satisfaction and fame to those who accomplished them, as well as to
the countries of which they were citizens. It became quite obvious that
the Northwest Passage transited by Amundsen and the *Gjøa* would not
be of any value for future maritime shipping, which was the original
reason behind the search for the Passage. It is too shallow and narrow
to accommodate large ships. Amundsen's exploit remains none the
less remarkable and it finally closed the centuries-old chapter on the

search for a Northwest Passage that had started with the Strait of Anian in the year 1500.

There is, however, a number of potential Northwest Passages other than the one transited by Amundsen. The one that holds the most promise for future shipping is through Lancaster Sound, Barrow Strait, Viscount Melville Sound (collectively known as Parry Channel) and finally Prince of Wales Strait. This is the one that was first transited by Henry Larsen in the *St. Roch* in 1944 and later by the American oil tanker *Manhattan* in 1969. This route will most likely be the first Northwest Passage to become practical for shipping as global warming continues thinning the Arctic sea ice.

The Norwegian explorer, far from resting on his laurels after sailing the Northwest Passage, went on to new exploits that brought Norway and himself further fame in the field of polar exploration. Undoubtedly the best known of these was his discovery of the South Pole on December 14, 1911, which had both its heroic and its tragic elements.

On October 19, 1911, Amundsen and four companions set out from the shore of Antarctica headed for the South Pole by dogsled. The English explorer Robert Falcon Scott[22] and eleven companions also set out for the Pole five days later from a different location and on a different route. For the final assault on the Pole, Scott had pared his team down to himself and four companions. He did not use dogs, but relied on motorized sleds and ponies, and, when these proved impractical, his team fell back on skis to continue. Scott and his four companions reached the Pole on January 18, 1912, only to suffer the bitter disappointment of seeing a tent flying a Norwegian flag mounted there which had been left by Amundsen about a month earlier after a trek of just under two months.

Scott and his men never made it back, dying of a combination of exhaustion, starvation and freezing to death. One of the most heroic deeds of polar exploration occurred on the way back when Lawrence Oates of Scott's team, with feet attacked by gangrene, could no longer stand the pain, and not wanting to compromise his companions' chances of survival, crawled out into a raging blizzard on March 17, 1912, his birthday, to face his death, saying as he left, "I am just going outside and may be sometime." His body was never found.

Robert E. Peary claimed to have reached the North Pole in March 1909, but recent studies have cast doubt on his claim and it is now widely felt that he did not reach the Pole. The honour of being the first man to reach the North Pole, if not actually setting foot on it, is now widely thought to belong to American aviator Richard E. Byrd who claimed to have flown over the pole in a fixed-wing airplane on May 9, 1926. On Byrd's return to Spitzbergen (now Svalbard) after the flight, Amundsen was on the tarmac to greet him and offer his congratulations. Four days later, Amundsen himself overflew the North Pole from Spitzbergen in the dirigible *Norge* commanded by Italian General Umberto Nobile, and carried on to land at Teller, Alaska, near Nome.

But now, Byrd's claim to be first to the North Pole (since Peary's claim has been discredited) is also being assailed. One of his early associates, Bernt Balchen, claimed after Byrd's death in 1957 that his flight to the North Pole was a hoax. More recent evidence seems to corroborate Balchen's claim, and, if proven, could mean that the honour of first person to the North Pole would then pass to Amundsen giving him a triple crown of first through the Northwest Passage, first to the South Pole and first to the North Pole, albeit not landing at the latter. This, however, remains to be seen.

It is perhaps fitting, though tragic, that Amundsen should end his life while flying on a rescue mission in the North. The Italian Umberto Nobile had crashed his dirigible near Spitzbergen and Amundsen was flying to lend his assistance to rescue him when his French Latham aircraft disappeared into the sea on June 18, 1928, somewhere between Tromsf and Spitzbergen, probably in the vicinity of Bjfrnfya (Bear Island). Some mini-sub searching was done in the area in 2004, but nothing was found.

Amundsen is a most highly revered national hero of polar exploration in Norway, along with Fridtjof Nansen and Otto Sverdrup.

CHAPTER NINE

Nechilli Inuit, The Sequel

AMUNDSEN CALLED THE INUIT WHO GATHERED around his ship at Gjøahavn "Nechilli Eskimo;" Henry Larsen called these same people "Nassilimmiut" in his book *The Big Ship*; today the accepted name for them in writing is "Nattilingmiut." These three different names are the result of attempts by owners of different sets of European ears and brains to render Inuktitut sounds in writing. The first part of the three expressions, *Nechilli*, *Nassili-*, and *Nattiling-*, mean "seals," whereas *-miut* means "people of the." Hence all three expressions mean "people of the seals."

In his book *The North West Passage*, Amundsen wrote, "My sincerest wish for our friends the Nechilli Eskimo is, that civilization may never reach them." More than sixty years later in 1967, a Canadian of Norwegian birth, Henry Larsen, reporting on the same group of Inuit had the following to say about changes wrought by civilization on the Inuit in the region of King William Island:

More and more people followed in the footsteps of the early Arctic explorers and the lives of the Eskimos underwent a complete change. Some say that these children of Nature are better off today than in the olden days, others claim that civilization has brought them only misery. The Eskimos themselves make no comment. Fatalistic as they are, I suppose they say "Ajurnarmat" (it can't be helped, that's life).[23]

There is a problem that modern civilization has yet to come to terms with, but to which the Inuit of old had found an effective solution – that problem is how to exit this world when life has becomes so painful to live that one wishes to die. The custom of assisted suicide when requested was well entrenched in the culture of the Nattilingmiut. By Larsen's time, the advance of the white man's culture in Inuit lives, however, had deprived them of access to this solution resulting in unnecessary pain and suffering. In 1937, Larsen became aware of a case of assisted suicide among the Nattilingmiut of King William Island, which he had to investigate. It is clear from what he wrote in *The Big Ship* that he fully sympathized with views on both sides of the divide on the issue of assisted suicide. He took a most humane position on this question.

> While I fully believed in this story and understood the circumstances, our laws nevertheless said that nobody could assist another in committing suicide. On this point the Criminal Code was quite clear, but I had no intention of letting this get any further or to have any of these people appear in a court, at least not if it was up to me.

Twelve years later in 1949, however, another case of assisted suicide among the same people turned out quite differently. A young man was sentenced to one year in prison at Cambridge Bay, with parole to be applied after four or five months, for helping his aged mother, apparently dying of tuberculosis, exit this world when she asked her son for his assistance. "Civilization" had advanced.

Amundsen was right to be concerned when he wrote, "My sincerest wish for our friends the Nechilli Eskimo is, that civilization may never reach them." The irony of the situation, though, was that he himself was the vanguard of the very civilization he feared.

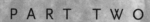

PART TWO

Henry Asbjorn Larsen and the St. Roch, 1940–44

A man in coat of ice arrayed
Stood up once by the Arctic Ocean.
The whole world shook with proud emotion
And Honour to the giant paid.

– Bjørnstjerne Bjørnson, "Post Festum"[1]

CHAPTER TEN

The Early Years

NO BOOK ABOUT THE NORTHWEST PASSAGE would be complete without the story of Henry Larsen's transits of the Passage in both directions between 1940 and 1944 in his famous RCMP schooner, the diminutive *St. Roch*. Seen through Inuit eyes, though, the *St. Roch* was far from being a small boat. The Inuit called Larsen *Hanorie Umiarjuaq* – Henry with the Big Ship.

Henry Asbjorn Larsen was born on September 30, 1899, on Herffl, an island in the Hvaler group of islands in Ostfold County, located in extreme southeast Norway. It is not far from the hamlet of Borge from which Roald Amundsen hailed some years earlier. Living next to ocean waters in his early years, Larsen developed a great love of the sea, the mists of which seeped into his soul, eventually dominating his life. While still in school, many of his holiday hours were spent aboard various types of small vessels – pilot boats, pleasure boats, fishing smacks – anything to get salty breezes blowing through his hair. Larsen heard the siren call of the polar regions while still at school, reading, as all good Norwegian boys did, of national heroes and Nordic polar explorers: Fridtjof Nansen, Roald Amundsen and Otto Sverdrup. Canadian Vilhjalmur Stefansson did not escape his attention either.

At the age of 15, Larsen first went to sea on a boat skippered by his uncle. This first adventure was not very exciting as it was limited to plying the waters between Norway and other Scandinavian ports in Denmark and Sweden, delivering shipments of lumber, fish and cobblestones. Larsen needed a wider horizon and he was not long in expanding it. Leaving his uncle's boat, he shipped out on truly international ships that went farther afield.

On his first international voyage Larsen quickly received a lesson on what sailors should not do. When he was clearing the harbour of Brest, France, aboard a real seagoing ship headed for Pensacola, Florida, rough seas ferreted out a couple of stowaways in the shape of two French girls thirsting for adventure but wracked with seasickness. The captain was not exactly pleased at the discovery, and the girls' would-be benefactors, two sailors who had definite plans for the girls, didn't have to wait long before they were cringing under a withering tongue-lashing from the captain in three languages that exhausted his repertoire of colourful words. The ship turned around immediately, and with signal flags flying, recalled the tugboat that had just left her. She delivered the seasick girls to the tug's captain to put them ashore, which he did to the tune of colourful, ungentle remarks about their ancestry. These unusual manoeuvres did not go unnoticed by French war vessels in port, which steamed urgently toward the returning ship thinking that she was under attack by a German submarine. It was 1915 and First World War was raging. This "rescue" by the French ships did not exactly smooth over the Norwegian captain's feelings toward his two enterprising crew members and their willing damsels. Undoubtedly, the pair of sailors became less than favourite members of the captain's crew.

It didn't take long for the reality of sailing in those days to set in for Larsen. As a still growing boy, Larsen was less than impressed with the quality of the meals he was served. The menu sounded like a recipe for scurvy – hardtack, sugar, salted meat and dried fish. And to top it all off, he had to share these meagre rations with an army of cockroaches. What probably saved the seamen from scurvy was the opportunity to add fresh fish to the menu by catching small tunas on a line dragged behind the ship.

In 1917, after several months of sailing between South America and New York, Larsen was back in Oslo with no prospects for work on shore, so he did what he knew best – he put out to sea again. He sailed southern seas once more, this time heading for Montevideo, Uruguay. He was there in November 1918, when all the church bells in the city started pealing at the same time and hordes of shouting and singing people clogged the streets and dock area. The First World War had finally ended, but the fighting was only beginning in the taverns and pubs of Montevideo, as drunken sailors from the nations of the world put the finishing touches on the hostilities between countries.

In February 1919, on his way home to Oslo, Larsen was shipwrecked on the American coast near Charleston, South Carolina, during a 24-hour hurricane. Though this interruption did not change his plans to get home, it did put a major detour in his homeward itinerary. He shipped out of Charleston on his first steamer ever, the *Vinstra*, which was powered by coal instead of wind, reaching Norway via Cape Town, Java, Ceylon (now Sri Lanka), Aden, Suez, Port Said – none of which impressed him favourably – then Gibraltar, Rotterdam and finally Oslo.

In an effort to broaden his skills, since his considerable experience in sailing ships would soon no longer be prized due to the rapid disappearance of this type of vessel, Larsen entered the Norwegian State Navigation School from which he graduated in the summer of 1920. This qualified him to navigate steam as well as sailing ships anywhere in the world. Like all other fit, young Norwegian men, he had to do his military service and so joined the navy for a compulsory two-year stint. In 1922, his responsibility fulfilled, Larsen signed on as fourth mate aboard a Norwegian Motor Ship, the *Theodore Roosevelt*, and embarked on a series of four round-trips to Hawaii and the west coast of North America. It was on one of these trips that Larsen met polar exploration hero, compatriot Roald Amundsen, who came aboard the *Theodore*

Christian Klengenberg, his Inuit wife Gremnia, and their Inuit family
Courtesy of Library and Archives Canada, E-002280198.

Roosevelt in Seattle. This chance meeting with the first navigator of the Northwest Passage fanned Larsen's smouldering interest in the North into a flaming passion. Larsen wrote in his autobiographical book *The Big Ship*, "We had no crystal ball in my cabin in the *Theodore Roosevelt*, but one thing I did know: I had to get to the North. In spite of a promotion to Third Mate and the promise of a good career with the shipping line, I made up my mind to give it all up in order to realize my dreams."[2] Very much like Amundsen, once Larsen set his sights on somehow ending up in Arctic waters, he embarked on a course of action and followed it unerringly until it took him there.

Although the most crucial element that eventually got Larsen into the North was his single-mindedness about getting there, luck was also an important ingredient. He left the *Theodore Roosevelt* in Vancouver in 1924 to pursue his "Northern Grail" and, by chance, read a newspaper article about one Christian Klengenberg[3] from Coronation Gulf, a body of water that separates Victoria Island from the Canadian Arctic mainland. Klengenberg had come to Seattle at that time to purchase a schooner to return to his home in the Arctic. Larsen lost no time in heading for Seattle harbour and where he began looking for Klengenberg's schooner, the *Maid of Orleans*, which was said to be berthed there. He soon found her and introduced himself to the old, white-haired captain and the two young men aboard. They turned out to be Klengenberg and his two, part-Inuit sons. The old man and Larsen hit it off and Klengenberg quickly hired the Norwegian since he was in need of a licensed navigator for his trip back home to his Inuit wife and the rest of his considerable family living on Victoria Island. Klengenberg was on his first visit south of the Arctic in 17 years. It impressed Larsen that Klengenberg had met Amundsen and Stefansson when they had run into each other on Herschel Island in 1906, the year Amundsen finally headed south from nearby King Point after successfully conning the tiny *Gjøa* through the Northwest Passage. Klengenberg was a world sailor from Denmark who, in the 1890s, had stepped off a whaling ship in the Arctic and settled down with an Inuit woman on Victoria Island.

Once Larsen was hired on as the mate of the *Maid of Orleans*, he was immediately occupied making the two-masted schooner ready for sailing. Apart from the owner and his sons, Larsen and four others formed the crew. Klengenberg had loaded his ship with supplies of all kinds to trade with the Inuit, and with a total of eight men and one woman aboard, the *Maid of Orleans* headed north in June of 1924. The lone woman, the fiancée of the engineer, was going to teach the Klengenberg children. From Seattle, the schooner sailed west across the Gulf of Alaska, around the Alaska Peninsula and then north through Bering Strait to Point Hope on the coast of Alaska some 35 kilometres (22 miles) north of the Strait. Klengenberg was well known in Point Hope and there was great excitement about his unannounced visit. However, there was one person in the group of northerners who seemed to be somewhat of an outsider at Point Hope and indeed he was. He was the Greenlander, Knud Rasmussen, the famous half-Inuit ethnographer who had set out from Greenland in 1921 on his Fifth Thule Expedition, the main finding of which was that all Inuit across the whole Arctic effectively spoke the same language, albeit with relatively minor regional peculiarities. Amundsen had met him at Dalrymple Rock off the coast of Greenland in 1903 during the first year of his Northwest Passage voyage.

Charlie, as the people of the North knew Klengenberg, decided that running into Rasmussen, a Dane like himself, called for a major celebration of eating and partying. The celebration lasted two whole dizzying days after which the Inuit invited everyone to a dance that lasted many more frenzied hours. All good things finally come to an end, though, and the *Maid of Orleans* sailed northeast to Point Barrow and then east to Herschel Island, running into thick fog and ice that made the trip somewhat more exciting and dangerous.

For years, Paulin Cove on Herschel Island had been a favourite refuge for American whalers stopping over and, in many cases, spending the winter ashore. Although the island was squarely north of the Canadian mainland, the government in Ottawa had never established the rule of law there. Consequently, degrading alcoholic and sexual orgies had dragged the local Inuit population down to the often diseased whalers' level of drunken stupor. Canada finally did step in when her sovereignty in the Arctic was suddenly and seriously threatened by the Norwegian *Fram* expedition under Captain Otto Sverdrup, which claimed a large area of the Canadian Arctic for the Norwegian government in 1902. The very next year, in 1903, the Royal North West Mounted Police (precursor of the Royal Canadian Mounted Police) quickly created two police detachments in the western Arctic, one of which was on Herschel Island. From that time on, the RNWMP/RCMP has enforced the law on the Island, ending the previous wholesale debauchery.

The presence of the RCMP however, did not protect Larsen from the danger of losing his bachelorhood. He was still wearing the uniform of his last ship, the *Theodore Roosevelt*, all navy blue and shining with brass buttons, topped with an officer's cap balanced on his head. His impressive get-up was not lost on an Inuit woman from the east who had come to Herschel Island for matrimonial purposes, and Larsen looked like a very desirable candidate to her. The Norwegian politely declined, gently letting the lady know that he was not quite ready for marriage yet.

For the next two years, Larsen piled up his Arctic sailing experience during two stints with Klengenberg and his schooner, interrupted by a round trip to the tropics on another ship while the *Maid of Orleans* was being refitted. At the same time, the vessel changed names to become the *Old Maid* as another ship was already registered in her original name. In May 1927, while in Vancouver on other business, Larsen applied for Canadian citizenship which he was granted on November 18, 1927. He was now one step closer to his burning desire, more determined than ever to stay in Canada and one way or another to get up into the Arctic. What really excited him was the news he received, when in Vancouver, from a friend of his, Corporal Pasley of the RCMP. The force had definitely decided to have a ship built the following year, 1928, for the specific purpose of patrolling northern waters and Pasley had been chosen to command her. To make Larsen's dream complete, Pasley told him that he wanted him as a member of the crew. Larsen's next step was clear. He had to apply and be accepted as a member of the RCMP. A few weeks into the new year Larsen applied and shortly afterwards, was summoned to present himself to the Vancouver Detachment. It was April 16, 1928 and he was in! Thus began a new and defining phase of his life.

CHAPTER ELEVEN

The St. Roch

LARSEN'S FRIEND, CORPORAL ED PASLEY, HAD THE
task of supervising the building of the new Arctic patrol vessel under
the orders of Captain Gillen of Newfoundland, who had previously
skippered a whaler operating in Bering Strait.

The RCMP vessel was built in the shipyard of the Burrard Dry Dock
Company of North Vancouver. Her design took advantage of hard and
tragic lessons learned from the loss over the years of dozens of wooden
whaling ships and their crews to the irresistible crushing pressure of
Arctic sea ice. One of the first shipbuilders to profit from these lessons
had been Norwegian Colin Archer, the designer and builder of Fridtjof
Nansen's schooner *Fram* in the late 1800s. The reason so many
wooden ships were crushed by the irresistible force of ice was almost
invariably because their sides were virtually vertical. Nansen and
Sverdrup had recognized this deadly factor in the loss of many whaling
ships that were being nipped and crushed by the tremendous lateral
pressures that sea ice generates. These lessons influenced Archer to

design the *Fram* with curved, sloping sides, forming a hull somewhat in the shape of a salad bowl. Such a configuration redirects the force of lateral ice pressures to squeeze a ship safely upward, rather than crushing it. From that time on, many ships used for polar exploration were built with the salad bowl design. Examples include Amundsen's *Gjøa* and later his *Maud,* and Captain Bernier's *Arctic.* It was a design made popular by the Norwegians.

Famed Canadian Arctic skipper Joseph Elzéar Bernier of L'Islet, Québec, was one of the first sea captains to appreciate that straight-sided ships ran great risks of being crushed by sea ice, just three years after he had skippered his first ship across the Atlantic when he was seventeen years old. In 1871, in a dockyard on the Potomac River near Washington, DC, Bernier spotted C.F. Hall's ship, the *Polaris,* at dockside, being outfitted for Arctic service. With a critical and knowing eye, he examined her and declared that her sides were too straight up and down and predicted that she would be crushed by ice. His warning was ignored and the *Polaris* sailed off on her last trip, one from which she never returned, crushed and sunk by ice off the coast of Greenland on October 16, 1872. Before he went on his first northern mission in 1904, Bernier made sure that the ship he purchased in Germany for the purpose, the *Gauss,* had a bowl-shaped hull. She had recently proven her ice-worthiness on a voyage to the southern polar region. Bernier bought her and sailed her to Canada, renaming her the *Arctic.* The schooner being built in the Burrard Dry Dock for the RCMP also had a round bottom, which, though it was great protection against being crushed, was also a guaranteed recipe for seasickness. The round hull greatly accentuated the tendency of a ship to roll in rough seas.

The schooner slid down the ways into Burrard Inlet in May 1928 and was christened *St. Roch* in honour of Ernest Lapointe, then Minister of Justice, whose electoral riding was St. Roch in the Province of Québec. Built 98 feet long with a beam of 25 feet, she displaced 645 tons. Her hull was of Douglas fir, sheeted overall with Australian gum-wood (also known as ironwood), an extremely hard wood to protect the much softer fir from the ravages of ice. She accommodated thirteen men below decks in spaces that could not be called large. Her rudder

The *St. Roch* under-
way. *Courtesy of
Library and Archives
Canada*, PA-121409.

was also made of strong Australian gumwood and was set in a well that
allowed it to be raised on deck for repairs or for protection against ice
damage, much like the arrangements aboard Nansen's *Fram* and
Amundsen's *Gjøa*. As in the case of those two ships, the *St. Roch* has
been preserved, and is displayed in a special exhibit at the Maritime
Museum in Vancouver.

The *St. Roch* was to be crewed by nine men when she left on her
maiden voyage on June 28, 1928: captain, Ed Pasley; advisor to the captain, Captain Gillen (to leave the ship at Baillie Island Detachment –
Baillie Islands today); engineer, M.F. Foster (to be backed up by a temporary engineer as far as Baillie Island Detachment, provided by the
builders of the 150 hp diesel engine in Oakland, California); radio
operator, F. Sealey; cook, W.J. Parry; ordinary crew members, A.F.
Tudor, M.L. Olsen, T.G. Parsloe and H.A. Larsen.

Only three of the permanent crew members had ever been to sea
before – Tudor, Olsen and Larsen. That was the crew as planned, but
things didn't work out quite that way. Pasley had recently been married
and insisted on taking his wife on board with him. The RCMP didn't
quite see eye-to-eye with Pasley on this issue with the result that there
was a parting of ways, with Pasley withdrawing his services from the
St. Roch, and leaving the force shortly afterwards. The modified plan to

accommodate this unexpected development was put in place. The *St. Roch* would sail under the temporary command of Captain Gillen who would keep an eye on the performance of the other crew members on the trip and help decide which one would be the most appropriate to be named permanent captain once the *St. Roch* reached Herschel Island.

Larsen had played his cards right; how right, he was to find out a few weeks later. Just three months after joining the RCMP he was already on his way back to his beloved Arctic. On June 28, 1928, the *St. Roch* sailed out of Vancouver harbour north toward Prince Rupert, then almost due west across the Gulf of Alaska towards Unimak Pass at the western tip of mainland Alaska. It wasn't long before the *St. Roch* tested the landlubbers who were in the majority on board. With a northwest gale blowing in her teeth, she quickly displayed her tendency to roll and buck like a wild bronco. Even Larsen was impressed, "...though I was used to the sea, I must admit that this was as bad as anything I had ever seen. And yet I quickly came to love her and would never have traded her for any other." Seasickness quickly claimed all those who had never been to sea. Everything below decks became a soggy mess sloshing around in frigid sea water.

Finally the gale abated and the *St. Roch* continued sailing across the Gulf of Alaska to Dutch Harbour on Unalaska in Unimak Pass where she anchored. Her captain took the opportunity of a calm anchorage to clean up the mess caused by the gale and also took on supplies. The *St. Roch* then headed north along the same track Larsen had taken with Klengenberg in the *Maid of Orleans* a few years earlier, stopping once more in the community of Teller where Amundsen had landed with the dirigible *Norge* after departing Spitzbergen and overflying the North Pole two years earlier in May 1926.

Five weeks after leaving Vancouver, the *St. Roch* and her crew reached the port on Herschel Island and were surprised when not a soul came out to meet their ship. This was unusual since a vessel in port was usually an occasion for celebration. Then they noticed the quarantine flag flying. Finally, a very tired RCMP corporal rowed out to the *St. Roch* and explained what was going on. The Inuit of Herschel had been laid low by a fierce epidemic of flu which had decimated

Captain of the *St. Roch*, Henry Larsen
of the Royal Canadian Mounted Police.
Courtesy of Library and Archives Canada,
PA-121429.

them, but had not infected the white population. Thus, the few whites
had had to minister day and night to the sick and dying Inuit who
greatly outnumbered them.

Inspector V.A.M. Kemp, Commanding Officer of the western
Arctic was stationed at Herschel Island. He decided to join the *St. Roch*
as she sailed on east to inspect the Baillie Island and Cambridge Bay
Detachments, and also to observe the *St. Roch*'s crew while under sail
since he would be making the final decision in naming a member of
the crew to be captain of the *St. Roch*. At Cambridge Bay, the officer-in-
charge of the detachment, Sergeant Frederick Anderton, was taken on
board the *St. Roch* to be responsible for police administration for the
remainder of the voyage.

By August 28, the *St. Roch* was back at Baillie Island and Kemp was
ready to reveal who would fill the position of captain on the ship.
Kemp's words to Henry Larsen were, "As you know, Larsen, the most
important decision is to pick the skipper and chief navigator. I have
kept an eye on you on this trip and have decided to give the job to you.
First of all you know the waters around here better than anybody else
in the crew, and secondly, you have long experience at sea." Larsen's
dogged single-mindedness and persistence had paid off. He was to be
Captain Larsen from now on.

At the Baillie Island Detachment, work was started to make her ready for the coming winter. Fuel, supplies, dogsleds and dogs were loaded on board. It was only the beginning of September, but it was none too early for her to set out on her first cruise under Larsen as captain and settle into her winter quarters before ice conditions forced her into an unsuitable anchorage.

The men of the *St. Roch*'s crew when she went into her first winter quarters were: engineer, Jack Foster; second engineer, Bob Kells; mate, Frank Tudor; second mate, M.J. Olsen; radio operator, Fred Sealey; cook, W.J. Parry; seaman, T.G. Parsloe; police administration, Frederick Anderton.

Inspector Kemp had already decided that Langton Bay at the head of larger Franklin Bay on the Arctic mainland coast would be her home for the next several months until spring finally released her from her icy prison to continue on her maiden cruise. As if to test the ship and her men, a powerful blizzard arose when they were off Baillie Island, forcing Larsen to make his first important decision as captain regarding the welfare of his charges and their vessel. He considered it too dangerous to ride out the storm anchored at Baillie Island and chose instead to sail his ship away from land and into the open sea of Amundsen Gulf far from any dangerous shore. Not everyone on board felt comfortable with that decision, especially the landlubbers who reacted poorly to the rolling and bucking that their round-bottomed schooner inflicted upon them. In the depths of the screaming blizzard, some of them feared they would end their days in the wind-whipped waters of Amundsen Gulf. However, the storm lasted only six hours, not that long as Arctic blizzards go.

On September 5, when relative calm had returned, Larsen conned his ship south into Franklin Bay and on to *St. Roch*'s sheltered winter quarters in Langton Bay. There were still a few weeks left before ice locked the little ship up snugly for the winter, but it was wise to start winter preparations a little early. It would be the first Arctic overwintering for the *St. Roch* and every man onboard, except for Larsen who had had that experience with Charlie Klengenberg aboard the *Maid of Orleans*.

Preparations for the winter had progressed very well, so on September 23, Larsen took some time to go ashore in the ship's skiff with radio operator Fred Sealey to explore their surroundings on foot. The captain soon had cause to regret this move when a strong wind suddenly whipped up the waters of the bay. The two men immediately headed back toward their skiff, but found they could not launch it as the water level had dropped under the influence of the stormy east wind and the skiff was hard aground. Nor could the men aboard the *St. Roch* rescue Captain Larsen and his radio operator with the ship's motor launch because of the roiled up and swelling waves. "How could I have been so stupid as to leave the ship!" Larsen chastised himself. This was one of the very few serious lapses of judgment that the captain ever made in his twenty-year career sailing the *St. Roch* through dangerous and unpredictable Arctic waters.

The waters rose and the ship's anchors lost their hold. She dragged them, blown by the strong east wind toward the lee shore, a most dangerous position to be in. Fortunately, the bottom was fine sand which could not seriously damage the hull, but as the wind fell and the waters receded, the ship became good and stranded on its side on that shore and no amount of effort could nudge her toward open water. From experience in these waters, Larsen knew that his only hope was for a 180° shift of wind. A strong west wind would cause the waters to rise, and this time the force of the wind would be blowing the ship away from shore, and hopefully re-float the vessel.

Unfortunately, a calm settled down over that part of the coast at this time which was no good at all for freeing the ship. The west wind took its own good time in coming. Another factor came into play at this time. Sea ice would soon start forming and there was a danger the *St. Roch* would be immobilized on dry land in an impossible position to serve as home for her sailors – on her side, if a favourable wind did not show up. It was three anxious weeks after the stranding, October 14, before the west wind finally made its appearance, gentle at first, but then gradually stronger, enough to raise the water level. It took a lot of good hard labour including the temporary offloading of their heavy cargo of coal, but with the aid of the engine, the jubilant crew pushed,

Hoisting a walrus aboard to provide food for the
dogs. *Courtesy of Library and Archives Canada, PA-121388.*

pried and winched the *St. Roch* off the sandy shore and soon had her
solidly anchored offshore in a secure position to let herself be frozen
in. It had been a close call for the new captain and his ship.

There were many things to do before the *St. Roch* and her men were
ready to confront the long darkness, shrieking winds and abysmally
low temperatures that would soon assail their Arctic winter home. The
deck was covered with a temporary wood-and-canvas structure to provide working and exercise space within a protected environment.
Drinking water for men and dogs had to be procured. It was certainly
not going to be in liquid form at that time of the year. Large blocks of
ice were cut out of a nearby lake, enough to last the winter, and trans-
ported to the ship by dog team. Snow is an excellent insulating
material and enough snow blocks were cut to protect the ship and keep
it snug by lining the sides of the vessel from the surface of the sea ice
to the top of the main deck. The men had to catch a stock of fish for
feeding the dogs over the winter.

The ship may have been immobilized, but the men were not. There
were many police duties for them to carry out during the long winter.
Mostly, they were not the usual duties associated with police work for
the simple reason that there was precious little crime and sickness

among both Inuit and white who lived in this isolated area. The duties had more to do with keeping track of who was in the region to ensure that if someone was in trouble, they could be helped. Larsen and his crew were also responsible for collecting census data on the northern residents. Apart from the Inuit, there were white men of various skills in the vicinity of Langton Bay – trappers, traders, missionaries and others. Visiting was an important social activity during the cold months. Whites and Inuit mingled freely in their visits by dog team among the various outposts of humanity and the honours were reciprocated. With spring came warmer temperatures, long days and much visiting by the peripatetic Inuit. This certainly did not facilitate the census work.

May 8, 1929, was red letter day for the captain of the *St. Roch*. He received a radio message announcing that he had been promoted a rank on April 1. Lest he think it an April Fool's trick, the radio message was confirmed with the required pomp and circumstance by a letter signed and presented to him by Frederick Anderton, Sergeant, I/C Detachment, who, it will be remembered, was aboard the *St. Roch*.

> This is to notify you that on the 1st day of April 1929 you were promoted to the rank of Corporal in the Royal Canadian Mounted Police.
>
> Just to remind you that promotion has in the past been greeted by the simple method of buying drinks and cigars for all other members of the Detachment. As circumstances will not permit this at present, you are hereby advised that all members will be pleased to receive in lieu thereof a personal gift of $5.00 in cash, as a token of your good will, and personal behaviour in the future.

At the beginning of May, the *St. Roch* was stripped of her temporary winter covering of protecting canvas, which was no longer needed, although it would still be almost another two months before the ice released her grip on the little ship. On June 24 the ship floated freely in

The *St. Roch* iced-in for the winter at Tree River, Northwest Territories (Nunavut today). *From Across the Top of the World by James P. Delgado.*

the gelid sea water, but that did not mean she was free to go. Langton Bay was breaking up, but the ship was still exposed to the danger of huge floating ice floes that could easily do her in. Outside the bay, the sea was still mostly locked up in a layer of solid ice. This was a dangerous period for the *St. Roch*. The crew had to be particularly vigilant during this period as their ship was at the mercy of wind and currents that could crush her up against the unforgiving ice and sink her just as easily as if she had been on a lee shore. By manoeuvring carefully for two weeks in what open water he could find, Larsen managed to sail his ship into Herschel Island harbour. From there, he and his ship had to sail a two-week round trip to resupply a number of outposts in the area, and then it was home to Vancouver after racking up some 19,000 kilometres (11,860 miles).

For twenty years from 1928 until the *St. Roch* was retired from Arctic service in 1948, there was not one year that Larsen and the *St. Roch* did not sail Arctic waters. They made ten voyages to the Arctic during that period. On just three of them they did not winter in the north. On the seven others, Larsen and his ship spent one or more winters frozen into protecting harbours along some barren, windswept Arctic coast. The longest voyage of all without leaving the Arctic stretched from June 1930 to October 1934, more than four years. *The St. Roch*'s winter quarters for those four years was Tree

A Tree River Inuit girl loves her fish. *Courtesy of Library and Archives Canada, C-86437.*

River, some 145 kilometres (90 miles) east of Coppermine along the Arctic coast.

In the summer of 1937, on the way to Coppermine, the *St. Roch* and her men came very close to ending their days in the Arctic. She was not the first Arctic-going ship to receive the visitation of that most dreaded agent of destruction – a fire on board ship! Sverdrup in the *Fram* and Amundsen in the *Gjøa* had each been obliged to submit to trial by fire during their northern expeditions. Larsen and the *St. Roch* were not to be exempted.

One of the crewmen had just finished filling a 900-litre (200-gallon) fuel tank in the engine room and was letting out a few ounces of the fuel into a can from the valve at the bottom of the tank to clear out any accumulated sediment. Accidentally, he spilled some of it onto electric wiring and it immediately burst into flames, which leapt over to some oily rags nearby. The engine was running and theoretically could have powered the water pumps to douse the resulting fire. However, the control mechanism to switch the engine power from the drive shaft and propeller to the pumps was unreachable in the now flaming engine room. Next to the engine room, and sharing a common wall with it, was a locker holding 135 kilograms (300 pounds) of blasting powder. The one-inch common wall between the locker and the engine room was now on fire. The stage was set for an explosive and fiery *adieu* from this world for the *St. Roch*, Larsen and all his men.

The captain lost no time in organizing himself and his crew to combat the deadly situation. There were a dozen cans of fire extinguishing foam on board which Larsen and a crewman took turns activating and lobbing into the flaming engine room. Meanwhile, he mobilized his crewmen to rush and find as many blankets as they could, drench them in sea water and pass them on to Larsen and his helper to beat the flames down each time they threw a can of fire extinguisher into the inferno. Eventually the frantic men got the better of the flames and the fire finally subsided enough for the engineer to enter the smoking engine room and determine the seriousness of the damage was. Surprisingly, there was relatively little damage, much less than anyone could have expected given the flaming drama of the moments they had just experienced – just some charred woodwork and burnt paint on the fuel tank and the locker of blasting powder. It had been close, very close.

The RCMP was Canada's official presence in the north in those days and as such had a number of duties to perform in addition to counting the inhabitants. The few crimes, and particularly the very few murders, had to be investigated and the guilty parties taken aboard the *St. Roch* to bring them to justice at the nearest court of law. Sick people had to be taken to hospitals. Children were taken to schools away from home. Whalers and traders had to be supervised. Duties were collected from those of foreign countries. In effect, Canadian sovereignty in the Arctic was being reinforced.

Two of Larsen's Arctic trips with the *St. Roch* are noteworthy, especially with respect to the Northwest Passage. From 1940 to 1942, he became the first man to sail the Passage from west to east, from Vancouver to Halifax, and in 1944 he returned in the opposite direction by a more northerly route taking a short eighty-six days and becoming the first man ever to sail the Northwest Passage in one season.

CHAPTER TWELVE

The Great Assignment, 1940-42: From West to East

WHEN THE *ST. ROCH* AND HER MEN HAD departed Vancouver for the Arctic in 1938 the world was at peace though the drums of war rumbled in the background. When they returned in the fall of 1939 though, it was to a world in the initial throes of a war that would soon engulf the human race in a struggle, the likes of which had never been seen. His adoptive Canada herself was at war. Early in 1940 Larsen, who by now had been promoted to the rank of sergeant, was sent to Ottawa to take an advanced police course. He was not aware of any other reason for going to Ottawa, but there *was* one, a very important one, both for Canada and for Larsen personally. One day he was called into the office of S.T. Wood, commissioner of the RCMP, the head of the force, to discuss the *St. Roch's* next Arctic trip. This was not entirely unexpected by Larsen as Wood had been the driving force behind the launching of the RCMP Arctic patrol vessel and took a lively personal interest in her fortunes. But Wood's interest was at a significantly higher level than just personal this time; it concerned Canada's activities in her Arctic reaches at this critical time of war. What Wood had in mind for Larsen's next Arctic patrol suited the captain of the *St. Roch* to a "T."

The first part of his assignment was normal enough. He would have on board a full load of supplies, which the *St. Roch* would distribute to the detachments of the western Arctic to see them through the coming winter season. The next part was right along Larsen's line of thought about Canada's responsibilities regarding sovereignty; he was to keep enough supplies on board the *St. Roch* to then carry on eastward through the Northwest Passage on a top-secret mission, the purpose of which no one could have guessed.

In March 1940, Larsen returned from Ottawa to the naval shipyard at Esquimalt harbour near Victoria, BC, where the *St. Roch* was to be made ready for what he called the "Great Assignment." Although there was not that much to be done to her, the ongoing war had created a lot of business for the shipyard and Larsen had to stand in line with a number of other high priority ships' captains to get his vessel refitted. The most important item was the replacement of the iron sheathing that protected the bow. The new sheathing was applied in a way that made the bow much sharper than before, which was going to be very useful for knifing through thick Arctic ice floes.

Apart from Larsen himself, only a very small, and very select, group of people knew the real purpose of the *St. Roch*'s voyage. Not one of the crew members (with the possible exception of the mate and the engineer) was aware of the nature of the voyage on which they had embarked. They would not be told until their ship reached the Bering Sea port of Dutch Harbour in the Aleutian Islands of Alaska. At this point Larsen gathered his crew together and let them in on the real purpose of their mission: they were to sail through the Northwest Passage into eastern Arctic waters and head for Greenland for a wartime assignment. Every man on board was given the option of leaving the ship at this point if he did not wish to participate further in the mission. Every man chose to stay on board and continue on to Greenland.

Canada and Great Britain were at war with the European Axis countries in 1940, although the United States would not be drawn in until

December 1941 with the Japanese attack on Pearl Harbour. By early 1940 Denmark had already been defeated and occupied by German troops. Greenland was a Danish possession and there were fears in the Canadian government that Germany might invade Greenland as well. First of all, this was a bit too close to home for Canada to ignore. But another crucial element of a possible German invasion of Greenland was the fact that the Danish island was the world's only significant source of a mineral that was absolutely essential to the Allied war effort – cryolite. There was only one mine in the world at Ivigtut, Greenland, at the extreme southwest extremity of the island that produced the mineral in significant quantity. Cryolite was essential for the refining of bauxite into aluminum. At the time, there existed no practical method for synthesizing cryolite in sufficient quantities to satisfy the need for the aluminum so critical to the Allies for the building of war planes. Canada feared that a German occupation of Greenland would seriously endanger the continued capability of her air force and those of other Allied countries.

There was no tangible support possible for Canada from the United States to counter any German activity in the region since the U.S. would not enter the war until some twenty months later in December 1941. The Canadian government, under the leadership of William Lyon Mackenzie King, made a bold decision: since occupied Denmark was in no position to defend Greenland, a Canadian 250-man force composed of personnel from the army, navy, air force and RCMP would occupy and defend the huge island to protect the cryolite mine. The *St. Roch* would have an important role to play in this initiative. Canada's decision was top secret, of course, so very, very few people knew about it. One of those few who knew was Henry Larsen. The 250-man main Canadian force would be preceded by an advance party known as Force X, composed of 88 military personnel and 12 members of the RCMP as soon as possible. The RCMP contingent would consist of four men stationed in eastern Canada who would travel north with the military plus Larsen and his seven crewmembers aboard the *St. Roch* from western Canada through the Northwest Passage.

Finally the *St. Roch* was ready and she stood out of Esquimalt harbour on June 21, 1940, on her historic and hair-raising voyage through the Northwest Passage. She had eight men aboard: Captain Larsen; Fred Farrar, mate; Jack Foster, engineer; Dad Parry, cook; Albert "Frenchy" Chartrand; Patrick Hunt; Bill Peters; and Edward Hadley, radio operator. Chartrand, Hunt and Hadley had no seagoing experience; the latter two being from the prairies, had never even seen the sea before.

Before attacking the Passage itself, Larsen had to anchor at a number of RCMP detachments in the western Arctic to unload supplies, with the result that the *St. Roch* was only able to sail as far as Cambridge Bay by early September. Winter comes early in the Arctic and it soon became obvious to Larsen that with all the resupplying duties he had had to perform, there was not enough time left to make it through the Passage and reach Halifax in one sailing season. He headed for a safe harbour in which to overwinter, settling on Walker Bay on the west coast of Victoria Island. Larsen knew that Walker Bay would be a satisfactory place to anchor for the winter as the captain of the *Enterprise* had described it almost a century earlier when she had wintered there in her search for the Franklin expedition. By late September 1940 the *St. Roch* was soon snugly anchored and held fast by the rapidly forming ice. The crew set to it and made all the necessary preparations for winterizing the *St. Roch*, enabling her to survive the harsh winter in as safe and comfortable a way as possible. And, of course, that included obtaining drinking water in the form of blocks of freshwater ice.

Although the *St. Roch* had not been scheduled to stop over in Walker Bay, there would still be a lot of police work to do to keep the RCMP personnel busy patrolling the area and inspecting the Inuit communities on nearby Banks Island. Attempting the Northwest Passage would have to wait until the following year. One thing that greatly pleased Larsen was to find Charlie Klengenberg's Inuit widow, Gremnia, and children living in Minto Inlet just a short distance south of Walker Bay. Charlie Klengenberg had died nine years previously. The captain of the *St. Roch* thought very highly of the Klengenberg's who succeeded in raising their children to be very successful in the environment and times in which they lived. The couple managed to have their offspring learn to read and write while Charlie and the local

The captain's table aboard the *St. Roch.*
Courtesy of Library and Archives Canada, PA-121411.

Inuit taught them how to survive, teaching them the skills needed to live entirely as Inuit.

Christmas is usually a time of great celebrations in the Arctic with elaborate feasts, dancing for hours on end and much visiting between igloos and any ships that happen to be frozen in for the winter. Christmas 1940, though, was a great disappointment to the crew of the *St. Roch*. A huge Arctic storm with shrieking, tearing winds blew up making it absolutely impossible for anybody to even stick their noses outside, let alone move about between igloos and ship. The *St. Roch's* cook had prepared an unusual and delicious meal of small, northern owls, called *ookpiks*, which Larsen and his crew had to eat in rather quiet surroundings for a Christmas day in the Arctic.

By March 1941 Larsen judged that the deep, dark cold of midwinter in the Arctic had subsided enough for him and his men to start dogsled patrols of the region they were responsible for overseeing. On March 17, Larsen and an RCMP Constable plus an interpreter set out with two dog teams and loaded sleds headed across Prince of Wales Strait for Banks Island. The going was pretty rough even though they had picked up an Inuk, employing him to help them for part of the trip by driving the dog teams over the jumbled-up ice of the strait. Open water forced the expedition farther north than expected to make a safe crossing of the strait. The great weight of the sleds combined with heavy snowfalls made the travelling excruciatingly slow. It took a full two weeks to reach their first destination of Sachs harbour, which was some 240 kilometres (150 miles) away as the crow flies, averaging only about 18 kilometres (11 miles) a day.

Larsen had a high opinion of the Banks Island Inuit who were an industrious lot of skilled trappers, many of whom were considered wealthy earning $10,000 to $15,000 a year with their trap lines, amounts quite comparable to excellent salaries for skilled workers in the south at the time. Larsen considered the Bank's Island Inuit his friends. Not only were they wealthy, but also they earned their money strictly in accordance with the game laws in effect in the Arctic. However, there had been rumours that game laws were being broken by the Inuit of Banks Island, but the rumours were proven to be false in a coincidental way. Larsen's sled expedition arrived at Sachs harbour the day after the end of the trapping season and he found that the Inuit had removed all their traps from the trap lines and had stored them ready for the next season, even though the presence of the RCMP in the region had been unknown to the seven families of Sach's harbour Inuit. Larsen had not believed the rumours, and rightly so.

Inuit are renowned for being extremely resourceful mechanically, from fixing broken down skidoos with haywire on the trail at minus 45° C (minus 50° F) to, it appears, fabricating false teeth out of locally available material. Larsen ran into an old Inuit couple on Banks Island, Adam and his wife whom he had first met sixteen years previously. Itinerant dentists liked to work on Banks Island because the wealthy Inuit residents could afford costly dental work. Adam and his wife had each been fitted with false teeth some years back by a visiting dentist, but they were not happy with them. They couldn't chew very well with them, so Adam took matters into his own hands. Using the dentist-made set of false teeth as a rough guide and using musk horn as raw material, he carved out a set for himself and one for his wife. The homemade ones worked much better for eating, although his wife admitted that the professionally made ones were superior for smiling.

Albert "Frenchy" Chartrand (left) and Henry Larsen with some good-sized char. *Courtesy of Library and Archives Canada, E-003894954.*

In mid-May, on his last sled trip before the ice broke up, Larsen came pretty close to crashing through the ice with all the negative possibilities that that entails. He and one of his crew, Frenchy Chartrand, sledded out from Walker Bay onto the ice of Prince of Wales Strait to spot and explore some likely anchorages for future trips. That evening, the two travellers set up their tent on the ice just off a small island on the shore of the strait to sleep off the effects of a hard day's work. When Larsen woke up, he looked out the tent flap and was surprised to see a huge seal asleep on the ice almost within shooting distance. The seal was an *ujjuk*, or bearded seal, a type that can weigh up to about 500 kilograms (1,100 pounds). Some fine, fresh meat would be a welcome addition to the baked beans that were the usual fare on RCMP patrols when the men generally didn't have time to hunt for food. Larsen dressed quickly, but carefully so as not to alarm the seal and began stealthily stalking the dozing animal. It was essential to approach close enough to get in an accurate brain shot to instantly immobilize the beast, otherwise, in a split second the wounded animal could give a convulsive jerk and slip down into its hole in the ice and be lost forever to the hunter. Finally, at just less than 100 metres (325 feet) distant, Larsen aimed accurately for the brain, pulled the trigger and the seal never moved a muscle.

Larsen stood up and was all set to run over to the motionless *ujjuk* when he looked down at his feet and was stunned to see the bluish colour of a current of sea water rushing by just under the thin crust of snow. He quickly scrambled away to more solid ice and calmly surveyed the situation. The seal appeared to be on solid ice, but the problem was to get safely to it over the extremely thin ice separating the hunter from the animal. Larsen was willing to risk it, but only if he was secured to a line that Chartrand and the dogs could pull him out with if he broke through the ice. The plan the two men devised and put into action was the following: they unloaded a dogsled and Larsen took the empty sled and the still-hitched team of dogs over the thin ice and as close as he could to the seal – a sled can go over thin ice that a man on foot would break through. He then unhitched the dogs and turned them around so that they were facing away from the *ujjuk* and tied himself to a long line, the other end of which he attached to the unhitched, but still harnessed dogs who would pull him out if he fell through. Very carefully, he slithered on his stomach over the last metres of ice until he almost reached the seal, only to discover that the line was too short. But not by much. He took off his leather belt, carefully untied himself from his safety line and lengthened the line by using his belt. The free end of the belt now reached the large seal. Cutting loops in the tough hide of the *ujjuk,* he secured the end of his belt to the animal and climbed carefully onto its back. When all was ready, Chartrand knew what to do next. His loud shouting punctuated by the frightening snapping of the whip excited the dogs into straining with all their muscular strength, pulling the heavy load of Larsen-mounted-on-an-*ujjuk* swiftly over the thin ice to safety on the thick, land-fast ice floe.

That evening the two men celebrated their daring exploit with a well-deserved feast of delicious *ujjuk* liver.

It would be July before the *St. Roch* could break free of the ice that imprisoned her and continue on her mission through the Northwest Passage. That year, Larsen and his men were in an excellent position to make an early start into the relatively close Northwest Passage and sail all the way to Halifax before winter closed down the sailing season. It was with bitter disappointment that they learned by radio they would have to help distribute supplies to the various RCMP detachments in the region before sailing east. Due to the war, shipping was hard to come by, and the *St. Roch* would have to make her contribution to the war effort before continuing on their mission through the Passage. It might still be possible to get through the Passage, but the chances were getting slimmer.

One of the *St. Roch's* first ports of call for dropping off supplies was westward to Tuk-Tuk, or simply Tuk, as Tuktoyaktuk is commonly known by the locals. Anchoring there was tricky due to a strong off-shore current that made it necessary to use a special procedure for safely securing the ship at this moorage. First, the bow was secured to an anchor well embedded in the sea floor. Then the procedure required a few men from the crew to be on shore to catch a mooring line thrown from the stern of the ship, which was to be attached to an immovable object on shore. One of the men sent ashore for this manoeuvre was Frenchy Chartrand. He was extremely strong and, according to Larsen, he "often did two men's work." Chartrand had waded into the water and by himself grabbed the weighty line from the ship and ran it ashore before anyone else could help him, when he suddenly collapsed with sweat just pouring from his face and hands. He came around pretty quickly, though, and brushed the incident off as insignificant, but Larsen suggested he should consult a doctor about it. One was expected in the area soon, but Chartrand was adamant that he wanted nothing to do with a doctor because he might be sent "Outside" for further examination, and that would spell the end of Frenchy's participation in the *St. Roch's* mission. Besides, he appeared to have recovered completely from his momentary weakness.

When finished with his duties at Tuk, Larsen sailed his ship eastward reaching Coppermine, when it became evident that getting through the Passage that year was going to be pretty iffy. June and July were unusually calm which meant that the heavy ice did not break up and float away as it usually did under the influence of clearing winds. This left the way eastward difficult to navigate. Larsen still managed to con his ship through the ice all the way to Gjoa Haven, which was familiar territory for him. At this point, the captain thought better of his earlier gloomy predictions about reaching the east coast that year, and decided to try it. However, he didn't get very far before the unusually heavy ice became a serious drag on his ship. Larsen was nothing if not persistent. He bulled his ship past Gjoa Haven, turned north into Rae Strait and headed for Matty Island. He was aware that he was approaching the stretch of water that came pretty close to scuppering Amundsen's tiny *Gjøa* as she barely scraped over the shallow shoals of Rae Strait in 1903 in that stretch of the strait. Larsen had no plans to repeat Amundsen's nightmare with the *St. Roch*, which, being quite a bit larger than the *Gjøa*, drew considerably more water than the smaller vessel. In his book, *The Big Ship*, Larsen wrote of the night of September the 6, 1941:

> As the ice started to surround us, I backtracked a bit and proceeded to the Boothia shore, as close as I dared, and then anchored by a small rocky islet, not much longer than the ship. We had barely settled down when a strong snowstorm came up from the northeast. Both anchors were let out and we prayed that they would hold. We had the engine going most of the night, with huge ice-flows crashing down on us. With the engine we managed to turn some of the floes aside, but we were in constant danger, and all of us spent the whole night on the fo'c'sle peering into the darkness and the blinding snowstorm.

After a long and uncomfortable night parrying large, threatening ice floes that materialized out of the darkness and bore down on the ship, morning saw the northeast wind replaced by a south wind which drove the ship, together with the surrounding ice, to the north. This was the direction Larsen wanted to go in, but it would have been far safer without all that accompanying ice. After a second worrisome, uncomfortable night, some of the crew would have been relieved to see the *St. Roch* backtrack south and slip into the protective womb of Gjoa Haven to spend the coming winter, but Larsen didn't care to lose hard-earned,

Ice conditions confronting the *St. Roch* while navigating the waters of Pasley Bay. *Courtesy of Library and Archives Canada, E-003894953.*

already-conquered mileage toward achieving his objective. He was all for wintering as far north as possible, past the most difficult part of the Northwest Passage, the part of the Passage where Amundsen, his men and the *Gjøa* had come within a hair of leaving her timbers and the men their bones when they sailed through it in 1903 in the opposite direction.

The captain decided to seek refuge in Pasley Bay half way up the west coast of Boothia Peninsula where a protected inlet could serve very well for the expedition to spend the winter in relative safety, if only they could get there in one piece, which was not guaranteed by a long shot. The *St. Roch* sailed north, entered Pasley Bay and headed for the inlet. Larsen knew of the inlet's existence from sea charts of the area. At this point, the *St. Roch* entered the inlet, but soon found herself completely at the mercy of the surrounding drifting ice. She had no choice but to hope for the best as she was dragged helplessly along, going in whatever direction the thickly frozen layer took her.

> I wondered if we had come this far only to be crushed like a nut on a shoal and then buried by the ice. Then suddenly a larger ice-floe came crashing through the darkness and hit the side of the ship, making it list even more. She was practically on her beam ends [on her side] and it was our luck that the pressure did not

let up just then, but kept on as if by a miracle until the ship was pushed over and a few moments later floated on an even keel in deep water.

What seemed at first to be a respite was far from it. The wind was still pushing the *St. Roch* into an extremely difficult position hard against the eastern shore of the inlet. By skillful use of the ship's sea anchors together with wire lines secured to big rocks near shore, Larsen and his men successfully combated the worst the wild Arctic winds threw at them. Suddenly, the raging wind gave up the fight and a welcome calm fell over the inlet which allowed new ice to form, cemented in by the broken-up chunks of ice and the surrounding mush of snow and ice now transformed into fast ice, the *St. Roch* was trapped into what became her winter harbour. The following morning Larsen and his crew awoke to a dead calm under sunny, blue skies, a welcome change from the prevailing harsh winds of the previous days. Sailing further that year was now impossible, but at least the *St. Roch* was in a snug harbour and well positioned to reach the east coast the following summer.

The ship and her men settled down for the winter, taking care of all the chores that that implies, banking snow around the ship's hull to conserve heat, erecting a canvas covering for the main deck and getting in a supply of drinking water in the shape of blocks of ice. There were a number of Inuit camps in the region and one of Larsen's tasks that winter would be to gather information from the inhabitants for census purposes.

The *St. Roch* was in short-wave radio communication with a few well-established Arctic communities in the region such as Coppermine, Fort Ross and Gjoa Haven. From Gjoa Haven, Larsen asked that Inuit be sent to help with the sled trips that he and his men would have to take for the census. In the middle of November one lone Inuk hailed into camp in response to Larsen's request. To the captain's delight, he turned out to be Ikualaaq, an old friend of his whom he had met on a previous patrol of the *St. Roch* some years before. Ikualaaq had covered over 200 miles with only his dogs for company to answer

Hauling fresh water aboard the *St. Roch*, bucket by bucket. The water would have been obtained from icebergs and/or old sea ice, which loses its salinity with age. *Courtesy of Library and Archives Canada, PA-117812.*

Larsen's call. Before Christmas, Larsen and Ikualaaq set out from Pasley Bay on their first census trip, destination Fort Ross at the eastern end of Bellot Strait. At Fort Ross the post manager and his wife, Bill and Barbara Heslop, eagerly welcomed them. Visitors were not an everyday occurrence at Fort Ross, especially not visitors from the "Outside." On their way back, Larsen and his travelling companion visited a number of Inuit camps and asked the inhabitants a series of census-related questions that must have mystified them and made them doubt the white man's sanity. The two men returned "home" to the *St. Roch* in time for the Christmas festivities, which as usual, were greatly anticipated by the men locked into the Arctic ice for the winter and were well celebrated with huge feasts and gift giving. The world news that greeted Larsen was shocking and very worrisome – the outside world was engulfed in the flames of war brought on by Japan's sneak attack on the United States Navy at Pearl Harbour, an almost fatal blow that resulted in the entry of the U.S. into a conflict which was pitting the Axis countries of Germany, Italy and Japan against almost every other European country plus the USSR and others.

In early January, Larsen and Ikualaaq, accompanied this time by Frenchy Chartrand, set out on a second sled trip of some 320 kilometres (200 miles) or more to Gjoa Haven to the accompaniment of howling dogs, shouts and cracking whips. The purpose of the sortie was to establish a cache of food to help support the men of the *St. Roch*

Henry Larsen on winter patrol in the Arctic.
Courtesy of the Vancouver Maritime Museum.

on future census patrols in the region. They found the community and nearby Inuit camps in good shape. On February 13, shortly after the return of the Gjoa Haven patrol to the ship, some of the men of the *St. Roch* were busying themselves with a chore that not all them enjoyed. Frenchy Chartrand, however, took pleasure in this task, which was essential to the operations of the expedition – preparing dog food. All food was prepared ahead of time and frozen solid in meal-sized portions. When on patrol, there was no time to arrange meals either for dogs or humans, except for thawing out the food for the humans and sometimes for the dogs.

It was morning and Chartrand was on deck getting the stoves ready for cooking the food. He had complained of a small headache at breakfast, but that didn't stop him from carrying out his job. At this point, Larsen came up on deck, took one look at Chartrand and knew that something was very wrong with him. He sent him below decks to rest for a while. Frenchy was not there long before he collapsed while listening to the radio with his friends. Larsen was urgently summoned below, but soon after he got there, Chartrand was up, smoking a cigarette, recovered it seemed, and pronouncing himself well. Larsen went back on deck, but a few minutes later an urgent call sent him back below again, this time to see Chartrand in his death throes. He died soon after.

This was a heavy blow for the rest of the crew. Chartrand had been everybody's friend on board and was loved by all. He was the strongest man on board, and now he was dead. It was very hard to come to grips with the reality and finality of Frenchy's passing. The RCMP Superintendent of G Division, headquartered in Ottawa and to whom Larsen reported, was notified by radio of the sad event, and he in turn took it upon himself to personally visit Chartrand's parents to let them know that, sadly, their son had died while carrying out his duties aboard the *St. Roch*.

The question now was what to do about a proper burial and religious service for their beloved shipmate. In those days of relatively primitive transportation facilities in the Arctic, burial back home in Ontario would not have been possible before late the following summer after ice breakup and the arrival of the *St. Roch* on the east coast. Clearly, it was not feasible to take that route. The best that could be done for poor Chartrand and his parents was to give him a Christian burial in Pasley Bay accompanied by a proper religious service which meant the attentions of a Catholic priest, for Frenchy had been a Roman Catholic, the only member of the crew to be of that faith. Even that second-best option was not going to be easy to realize since the Catholic priest nearest to the solidly iced-in *St. Roch* in Pasley Bay was Oblate Father Henri Pierre who ministered to the Inuit of the Kellett River region near the present-day community of Pelly Bay, some 640 kilometres (400 miles) to the southeast. A complicating consideration was that before Father Henri could leave his mission to perform a burial ceremony in Pasley Bay, he had to find out that his services were required there. The only way for that to happen was for someone from the *St. Roch* to drive a dog team and sled the distance to Pelly Bay to let him know, and only then could Father Henri set out for Pasley Bay. It would be many weeks before poor Chartrand could be finally laid to rest with all due ceremony in his Arctic grave. A coffin was built for Chartrand's body, which was temporarily buried in a snowbank to await Father Henri's arrival.

Larsen, Ikualaaq and Constable Hunt began preparations for the long trip to summon the good Father. Food for about two months had to be cooked and frozen before leaving. There would barely be enough time while travelling to just thaw out the food, let alone cook it. Many dozens of doughnuts were fried up and frozen to take the place of bread. Beans, an important high energy staple, were mixed with bacon and other meat, usually canned bully beef or local game, canned tomatoes, onions, molasses, all seasoned with mustard and salt. After everything was boiled up into a thick stew, it was spooned into large pans and set out to freeze, then chopped up with an axe into smaller chunks and thrown into canvas bags for carrying on the sleds. For variety, the men also boiled up rice and potatoes together with other vegetables and meat. After cooking, these were put through a meat grinder. For liquids, canned soup and tomatoes were added in together with spices and the mixture was ladled out into flat patties and frozen. These were also put into canvas bags for transporting. Fixing up a meal was as simple as thawing out some chunks of beans and patties, plus a few doughnuts. Fish were also part of the menu. While hungry men were setting up camp, they chewed on chunks of frozen raw fish, which, curiously, have the quality of creating a sense of warmth and well being while waiting for the main course to be ready. Dog food consisted of fish and seal blubber or beef tallow to provide the fat that was essential for the hard-working beasts. The men expected that it would be up to two months before they returned to the *St. Roch*. They had better not run out of food for themselves or their dogs.

Fully aware of the police responsibilities his Arctic mandate entailed, Larsen planned his mercy mission as part of an official RCMP patrol for census taking. Although Pelly Bay, where Father Henri's mission was located, lay to the southeast of Pasley Bay where the *St. Roch* was locked in the ice, Larsen, Hunt and Ikualaaq started off on February 24 by first doing a loop to the northeast to include a good number of Inuit communities for census purposes before heading south to Pelly Bay. In heading northeast, Larsen was aiming for the Hudson's Bay post of Fort Ross at the east end of Bellot Strait where the post manager Bill Heslop and his wife Barbara were glad to welcome Larsen once more into their home. The patrol then continued north to Creswell Bay where there was a small Inuit community to count and include in the census. On this northern loop, the patrol passed Cape Garry, a place of great interest especially to Ikualaaq. While passing the cape, Ikualaaq drew Larsen's attention to what he claimed were remnants of very old dwellings built and used by a tribe of people long ago disappeared. Ikualaaq and his contemporaries had never seen these people, but he knew of them from legends passed down by his elders. These ancient people differed from present-day Inuit in that they had obviously been whale hunters, whereas modern Inuit in the same region were not. That these ancient people hunted whales was plain from the fact that their dwellings were constructed of whale bones and skulls. According to the legends, the Tunits, as these people were known, were supposed to have been of much greater stature than Ikualaaq and his contemporaries, which seemed to be confirmed by the huge whale skulls and large rocks that the Tunits had manipulated in building their homes.

Leaving Cape Garry, the expedition next turned south and headed for Kellet River where Father Henri's mission was located. On the way the patrol passed another area of legendary Tunit ruins at Cape Esther, then came to a large present-day Inuit camp complete with igloos, loose, roaming sled dogs and all the accoutrements of a camp except for one thing – people. Despite the usual uproar created among a camp's dogs on the arrival of a strange sled, not even one person stuck his head out of an igloo to see what was going one. This was strange indeed.

One of the igloos stood out among the others because of its size – it was huge compared to the others. Undoubtedly, it was an igloo built by the Inuit to enliven the long, dark days of winter with community activities such as drum thumping, singing, dancing, even physical exercise as Amundsen had discovered when he spent two winters in Gjoa Haven. As Larsen and his men approached the big igloo, they began to hear muffled noises inside that gradually resolved themselves into singing and strains of what sounded like an accordion. Larsen and his men dropped on all fours and crawled into the entrance tunnel of the Igloo to the door leading inside. From out of the opening door a cacophony of music and song blasted the visitors. They were met with a totally unexpected scene. The igloo was jam-packed with a large, entranced crowd of excitedly singing, sweating Inuit led in their expression of fervour by a giant of a white man passionately squeezing stimulating religious hymns from a concertina. No sooner had the three strangers stood up in the igloo, than the music and singing stopped as though cut off by a knife. The tall concertina-squeezing white man in huge polar bear pants was momentarily stunned at the sight of the strangers, especially the two white men. Who could they be?

When everyone had recovered from their temporary amazement, Larsen and his two companions introduced themselves to the leader of the celebration, who, it turned out, was Canon John Turner, a young Anglican missionary stationed in Pond Inlet. He was on his yearly tour of his widely-spread parish and was quite relieved to discover that the three visitors were not competing Roman Catholic missionaries. Men of the cloth in those days were very protective of their flocks, which were unprejudiced and quite open to the influence of missionaries from different churches. So heated was the competition at times that stories circulated of clergymen secretly hitching up their dog teams in the middle of the night to be the first to arrive at new, previously unvisited, Inuit communities, before their rival missionaries of other faiths could claim the people as members of their own church.

After the introductions, both sides being reassured of the benign nature of the other, the celebration picked up steam again with the Canon once more belting out religious hymns on the concertina, amplified by Inuit voices whose levels were set at the only volume they knew – top of the lungs. The vibrations from stamping feet and excited vocal chords, combined with the massive heat generated by the expenditure of so much human energy was too much for the structural strength of the huge igloo's roof – it collapsed on the celebrants. In typical Inuit fashion, what might seem a disaster to white people, was, on the contrary, an occasion for tremendous hilarity on the part of the Inuit who could hardly stand up, holding their stomachs with laughter. It was the funniest thing they had ever seen.

The singing might have been cut short, but the eating had yet to begin. Canon Turner cooked up a copious Inuit meal in his igloo where everyone ate until almost bursting. By the time the feast was over and the guests had sufficiently partaken of Canon Turner's hospitality, it was five o'clock in the morning. Larsen and his two companions finally lay down to sleep as did the Canon, but the churchman was soon up again to massage the Inuit souls to the tune of a morning service complete with wheezing concertina. Some years later, Canon Turner came to a tragic end when he accidentally shot himself in the head while returning from a hunting trip. He did not die immediately, but was carried back to his home camp where he lingered on until a mercy flight was able to land and speed him on to civilization for medical help, but it was too late and his horrible wound finally carried him off.

The next day, Larsen and his companions sledded on to the next major Inuit community, Thom Bay, where Larsen found what he called the finest and healthiest Inuit he had seen on this trip. Seals and fish were available in abundance in the area. On March 21, the RCMP patrol took a short side trip to Victoria Harbour to examine the last anchorage of Sir John Ross' ship *Victory*, abandoned in the ice in 1833. At this stage, Ikualaaq, feeling that he had been absent from his family long enough, decided it was time he returned home to Gjoa Haven which was a relatively short distance away at this point. He left the expedition after having provided excellent service as a guide to the expedition. Another Inuk named Kinguk, after consulting with his wife who agreed to the idea, offered his services and took Ikualaaq's place, guiding Larsen and Constable Hunt the rest of the way to Father Henri's mission on the Kellet River where it empties into Pelly Bay.

On arriving at Father Henri's mission, Larsen and his companions were given an especially warm welcome, typically offered by all northern residents to travellers who arrive at their doorstep, expected or not. Father Henri broke out a small barrel of frozen wine that the priest thawed out near the stove, enough to eke out a few glasses, which turned out to be plenty. The three visitors, dead tired from consecutive days of mushing their teams through frigid Arctic air were soon overcome with drowsiness and lay fast asleep where they fell, not to awaken till the following morning.

A snugly located travelling igloo by the light of the moon, with cracks lit by the fire inside. *Courtesy of Library and Archives Canada, E-004666358.*

Father Henri lived in a large house he had constructed himself of small stones embedded in clay. The priest was conducting morning mass when his visitors woke up, after which he prepared a substantial breakfast. It was soon to be Easter and Father Henri was expecting the annual sprouting of thirty-some-odd igloos around his house, an annual occurrence at that time as the Inuit from the surrounding distant camps arrived to take part in the Paschal celebrations. Such occasions called for enormous quantities of food and Father Henri was ready, having stocked up on layer upon layer of fish and seals that he had stored away in his commissary. Holidays such as Easter and Christmas were not treated lightly in the north. They were a great source of pleasure for both whites and Inuit. The Inuit, particularly, appreciated the celebration of these holidays as being one of the more important gifts conferred on them by missionaries.

By Easter morning, April 5 that year, the usual village of snowy mounds had grown up around the mission, temporary homes to the 80 or so worshippers that gathered in Father Henri's little stone chapel to benefit from spiritual and corporal sustenance. The priest's alter was flanked by a heap of thawing fish on one side and a great pot of seal meat simmering over a seal oil lamp on the other, occasionally tended to by the missionary as he said mass. The Inuit enthusiastically belted out hymns with old familiar religious tunes accompanied by lyrics of aboriginal origin. A young woman next to Larsen fell unconscious near him. He took her outside to revive her in the cold air and brought her back inside. Twice more she fainted and twice more Larsen revived her. It turned out that she had given birth just three hours before. Once the mass was over with, the feast began. Inuit were capable of putting away prodigious quantities of food when they put their minds to it. The White men were no slackers either, as their travel-whetted appetites were still quite sharp. Easter of 1942 was a great success for all – Inuit, white men, Protestants and Catholics.

Larsen informed Father Henri of the purpose of his visit, to ask him if he would come to Pasley Bay and conduct a proper Catholic ceremony for Frenchy Chartrand's burial. The priest was impressed by the considerable efforts undertaken on the part of the Protestant captain and his crew to see that their shipmate received the ministrations and blessings of a man of the cloth of his own Catholic faith. He was willing to undertake the long trip, but would have to wait a while until later in May, to set out when seals had begun showing themselves again on top of the ice. It would be necessary for the priest and his travelling companions to hunt seals for food along the way both for themselves and their dogs.

After six days of generous northern hospitality extended by Father Henri, Larsen and Constable Hunt headed back north to regain the *St. Roch*, stopping in at Gjoa Haven on the way. They were fortunate to have an Inuk from Pelly Bay accompany them since both Larsen and Hunt had caught bad colds that turned into a flu. They were very weak by the time they reached Gjoa Haven on the 15th of April. It took two weeks for the two men to recover enough to continue on their trip to Pasley Bay, finally arriving there on May 6. The patrol had taken seventy-one days to cover 1835 kilometres (1140 miles) of snow and ice. True to his word, Father Henri arrived at the *St. Roch* thirteen days after Larsen and preparations were begun for the burial. The Requiem Mass was conducted on board ship by Father Henri with Larsen, his crew and a number of Inuit in attendance. Chartrand's coffin had been laid to rest in a shallow grave on top of a nearby hill. It had not being possible to dig a deeper grave because of the rock-hard frozen soil. After the Requiem mass, a funeral procession climbed the hill to the grave where Father Henri pronounced final words of blessing over

Crew members cutting the *St. Roch* out of the ice to hasten the spring release. *Courtesy of Library and Archives Canada, PA-121392.*

Chartrand's body with all due solemnity, sprinkling the grave with a handful of snow rather that the usual holy water. Albert Chartrand's parents in Ottawa would be comforted to know that their son had been buried and blessed by a Catholic priest.

His mission accomplished, Father Henri and his three Inuit travelling companions embarked on their long return journey to his little parish on the Kellet River. He carried with him a solid hardwood cross built and presented to him by Larsen and the crew of the *St. Roch*. It was Larsen's idea to present the priest with a substantial cross as he had noticed the one Father Henri had at his mission on the Kellet River was made of pieces of wood from a packing case. How ironic, but appropriate, that the new cross in Father Henri's Catholic mission had been built and donated to the mission by a shipload of Protestants. Later that summer, Larsen and his men built a memorial cairn of stones over the grave to which was attached a brass plate with Chartrand's name and the dates of his birth and death inscribed on it.

During the summer, a young newly married Inuit couple, Teeirkta and his 16-year-old bride Evalu approached Larsen and asked to be taken aboard the *St. Roch* when she continued her voyage eastward. They wanted to be let off at Pond Inlet to meet Canon Turner. Although they had been married according to the Inuit culture, they still wanted their marriage to be sanctified by the Anglican Church.

In the middle of the night on August 3, there were signs the ice was breaking up. Larsen quickly took aboard everything that was on shore and prepared to move as soon as he was able to. He aggressively took advantage of every bit of open water to move out of Pasley Bay, risking the rigours of the breaking-up ice rather than the possibility of remaining locked in the bay yet another winter. As soon as he felt his ship break free – she had been icebound eleven months – Larsen started up his engine and forced the *St. Roch* forward some 25 kilometres (15 miles) through broken-up chunks of ice before his ship was once more immobilized as the lead closed and trapped her as solidly as ever. At least they were 25 kilometres to the good. The tremendous pressure of the ice pack bodily lifted the ship up over a metre (about four feet) and shook her from side to side as the men set off explosions of gunpowder to relieve the pressure. Ice was chiselled away from the rudder and the propeller to protect them from damage, which would have been disastrous. Larsen took advantage of every bit of open water that presented itself to advance his ship, back and forth, forcing his way. The wear and tear on the ship manifested itself quite dramatically on August 12, when a cylinder head in the engine cracked and stopped the engine cold. The piston in that cylinder was removed and from then on, the ship had to rely on the five remaining cylinders. Her maximum speed was reduced to little more than a brisk walk.

From anchorage to anchorage the *St. Roch* advanced northward when she could until, on August 29, she was at the mouth of Bellot Strait. The entrance to the strait was clear of ice and the *St. Roch* slipped in even though there seemed to be an impassable barrier of ice some distance ahead across the narrow strait. It was only 30 kilometres (18 miles) from the western to the eastern end where Fort Ross was situated and hopefully clear sailing was to be found, but these kilometres turned out to be some of the most dangerous yet faced by the little ship. The tide was behind the *St. Roch* and she was carried along bodily, accompanied by chunks of ice in the direction Larsen wanted to go, but what would happen when the ship reached the solid barrier of ice in the middle of the strait? With the tide behind them there was only one way to go – forward.

Larsen commanded his crew to ram the ship into the ice. Again and again and again the solidly built little ship smashed into the ice without too much visible effect. Then someone noticed that the current in the strait ran eastward on the southern shore while on the northern side it travelled in the opposite direction. It became obvious to Larsen and his men that they were contending with a huge whirlpool that had the power to suck the tiny *St. Roch* down into its watery maw. The whirlpool was caused by contrary tides coming into the strait from east and west and meeting in the middle. Again and again the captain commanded the ship to crash into the ice barrier while the young Inuit couple prayed continuously for the *St. Roch* and her human cargo. Suddenly, almost anticlimactically, the ice gave way and the ship was flung into clear and quiet waters and, carried along by the eastward tide on the southern shore, the icy trials and tribulations of Larsen and his companions were over. All the while, people from Fort Ross had been watching the desperate struggle of the *St. Roch* from a high hill in back of the trading post. When they saw that the ship was safe, Bill Heslop and his wife rowed out to meet the *St. Roch*. Climbing aboard the ship, they welcomed the men and their two Inuit passengers. A highly appreciated hearty meal prepared by Mrs. Heslop was waiting for them on shore. As Larsen put it, "Now we felt we had made it and were practically in Halifax."

After spending two days with the Heslops at Fort Ross, the *St. Roch* sailed on her way, slipping north along the coast of Somerset Island where there were some open leads in the otherwise ice-choked Prince Regent Inlet. Shortly before reaching Lancaster Sound, the *St. Roch* cut eastward across Prince Regent Inlet and entered the sound, heading for Navy Board Inlet and Eclipse Sound, to finally anchor in front of the RCMP detachment at Pond Inlet. It was at Pond Inlet that Larsen welcomed aboard Constable Jack Doyle who was the replacement for the opening left by Frenchy Chartrand's death. It was also in Pond Inlet that the young Inuit couple disembarked to finally meet Canon Turner who would officially sanction their Inuit marriage, complete with all the proper ceremony according to the Anglican Church.

At this point of the voyage, the original plan had been for the *St. Roch* to sail from Pond Inlet, east into Baffin Bay, and then south along the coast of Greenland to Ivigtut and the cryolite mine to assume occupation duties on the Danish island. However, back in April 1940, about a month before the *St. Roch* left Vancouver, the Americans found out about Canada's plans to occupy Greenland and reacted in a manner entirely unexpected by the Canadian government. President Roosevelt made it known to Prime Minister King in a meeting with him that under no circumstances was Canada to occupy Greenland. The U.S. secretary of State, Cordell Hull, invoked the Monroe Doctrine to support this intransigent position. Not wishing to displease the Americans, Prime Minister King quickly knuckled under and had Force X immediately demobilized.

However, the *St. Roch's* voyage had not been cancelled. Larsen had sailed as planned. The United States was not yet at war, so there was no guarantee that the Americans would protect Greenland from a German invasion. In this atmosphere of uncertainty, Canada could hedge her bets by allowing the *St. Roch* to continue her eastward trip with the options of heading for Greenland after transiting the Northwest Passage, or conversely, bypassing Greenland and sailing to directly to Halifax, depending on how the war had evolved in the meantime. As it turned out, Canada did not send the *St. Roch* to Greenland.

While the battered little ship was approaching Sydney harbour on Cape Breton Island, Larsen spoke to an official government naval patrol, which asked him the name of his ship plus where he originated from and where he was heading. Larsen replied by megaphone that the ship was the RCMP *St. Roch*, originating from Vancouver, destination Halifax. This information evidently flummoxed the young navel officer. He countered, "Well, you're a long way from your course. This is Sydney." Larsen replied to him that he knew exactly where they were, and that they had come via the northern route. This explanation didn't seem to clarify things for the naval officer, but he finally let the *St. Roch* continue on her course anyway, probably shaking his head as he did so.

The following day, October 9, 1942, the *St. Roch* anchored at her final destination of Halifax, becoming the first ship ever to navigate the Northwest Passage from west to east. This exploit was to come to the attention of King George VI, father of Queen Elizabeth II, who honoured Larsen and his crew by awarding each of them a Polar Medal, including their late shipmate, Frenchy Chartrand. In addition, Larsen was promoted a rank to Staff Sergeant

After flying to the west coast for a much deserved leave of absence with his family in Vancouver and Victoria, Larsen returned to the East coast where his orders for the 1943 navigation season were to take the *St. Roch* on an inspection trip and a resupply mission to the RCMP detachments of the eastern Arctic. During the winter and spring following this trip, the *St. Roch* was given a thorough overhaul that included the replacement of her 150 HP diesel engine by one with double that power, as well as a redesigned mast arrangement as recommended by Larsen. The new engine could thrust the *St. Roch* along at a cruising speed of nine knots, three knots faster than when powered by her old engine. It was undoubtedly not a coincidence that these improvements were followed by the issuance of orders for Larsen to take the *St. Roch* home to Vancouver during the 1944 navigation season, again via the Northwest Passage.

CHAPTER THIRTEEN

Back Home Through the Northwest Passage, East to West, 1944

THE PRINCIPAL REASON GIVEN AT THE TIME
for the 1944 trip was the strengthening of Canadian sovereignty over
her Arctic islands. This time, though, the route followed would be
different. Instead of going through the narrow and shallow, ice-
choked Rae Strait that came close to fatally crunching the hull of not
only the *St. Roch*, but also of Amundsen's *Gjøa* before her, Larsen
chose a more northerly route through Lancaster Sound and west
through either McClure Strait or Prince of Wales Strait. It was anticipated that the trip might take two years to complete and the ship was
accordingly provisioned with food and supplies. Essential spares
such as an extra propeller and rudder were loaded on board. Up till
then in her career, the *St. Roch* had been lucky not to lose or damage
either of these essential pieces of hardware. It was best not to tempt
fate by taking chances.

The *St. Roch* stood out to sea from Halifax Harbour on July 19,
1944, destination Vancouver. Her crew of ten men of all ages included

the following: G.W. Peters, engineer, and P.G. Hunt, clerk and seaman (both of whom had crewed for Larsen on the east-west crossing of the Northwest Passage); J.M. Diplock, seaman; O. Andreasen, who was 65 and had explored with Stefansson, seaman; L.G. Russill, radio operator; R.T. Johnson, who was 60 years old, second engineer; W.M. Cashin, 17 years old, seaman; J.S. McKenzie, seaman; F. Matthews, seaman; and G.B. Dickens, cook. There was one additional man aboard, M.G. Owens.[4] Mr. Owens was a member of the RCMP on his way to Pond Inlet to take up Police duties there.

Within four hours of sailing on July 19, 1944, the *St. Roch* had to put about and make for Halifax for repairs to a defective cooling system. Three days after repairs, she once more pointed her prow west, but before long more defects flared up and the following day a potentially fatal one was discovered in the exhaust stack that could have set fire to the ship. The *St. Roch* turned tail again, this time towards Sydney, Nova Scotia, for more repairs before once more putting out to sea on July 26, but only to experience an overheating engine, which luckily was corrected by making some on-board adjustments. After topping up her fuel tanks at Curling Cove, Newfoundland, and adjusting a slipping clutch, the *St. Roch* pushed her snout against the Atlantic waves, destination Vancouver. It was not an auspicious start to a long and dangerous Arctic journey, but the repairs paid off – the expedition's ship remained mechanically trouble-free for the rest of the trip.

Larsen guided his ship north along the Labrador coast and up Davis Strait where she encountered the ice pack. When the ice proved to be a serious impediment to her progress, the captain conned his ship east toward Greenland where he found open water, and headed north in an end run manoeuvre around the top of the ice pack. He then steered the *St. Roch* west around the extremity of the pack and entered the relatively open water of Lancaster Sound, the beginning of the Northwest Passage. Fog and random ice floes off the coast of Baffin Island made for difficult and dangerous sailing until, on August 9, Larsen sighted Bylot Island. He entered Pond Inlet and anchored in front of the village and RCMP detachment of the same name. Here, Constable M.G. Owens was dropped off to take up RCMP responsibilities for his next tour of duty. It was also at Pond Inlet that the *St. Roch* picked up an Inuit family: Panippakussuk, along with his wife, mother, four children of his brother Kyak, fifteen-year-old Arreak, nine-year-old Anne, eight-year-old Mary, four-year-old Sophy, and seventeen dogs. This was quite an increase in human and animal passengers aboard, but the group did not disrupt the ship's routine since they insisted on living in a large tent raised on the ship's deckhouse rather than below decks. The women would sew clothing for the men, and Panippakussuk, or "Jo" as he liked to be called, would hunt for meat. He quickly demonstrated his skills by shooting a polar bear with Pond Inlet barely out of sight on August 20, the day the *St. Roch* departed.

The *St. Roch* stopped at Dundas Harbour on Devon Island to inspect the uninhabited buildings of the RCMP detachment that had operated there a number of years before and for which there might still be a use in the future. Larsen then carried on westward, looking in at historic Beechey Island on the way. Farther west, he anchored in Winter Harbour on Melville Island. It is here in 1909 that Captain Bernier left a bronze plaque anchored solidly into the large and prominent rocky face of Parry's Rock. The plaque is inscribed with a declaration of Canadian sovereignty:

> THIS MEMORIAL IS ERECTED TODAY TO COMMEMORATE TAKING POSSESSION FOR THE DOMINION OF CANADA, OF THE WHOLE ARCTIC ARCHIPELAGO, LYING TO THE NORTH OF AMERICA, FROM LONG 60 W TO 141 W, UP TO LATITUDE 90 NORTH. WINTER HRB. MELVILLE ISLAND, C.G.S. "ARCTIC." JULY 1ST 1909. J. E. BERNIER, COMMANDER, J. V. KOENIC, SCULPTOR.

From that time on Canada no longer considered it necessary to land on, and claim, each individual island of the archipelago. The plaque covered the whole Arctic north of Canada right to the North Pole.

Continuing westward through Viscount Melville Sound, Larsen tested the frigid waters of McClure Strait, but found them choked with an impassable jumble of broken-up ice pouring down from the north, as is the case practically every year. He turned the *St. Roch* around and headed southeast, entering the Prince of Wales Strait on the third day of September. The strait was mercifully almost clear of ice under a cloudless and sunny sky, a perfect day for sailing. About 275 kilometres (170 miles) in length, the strait narrows down in width to some sixteen kilometres (ten miles) with islands in mid-channel. The narrowness makes it impossible for foreign ships to pass without violating Canada's sovereignty, Canadian shores enclose the full width of the strait for several kilometres. With very little interference from ice, the *St. Roch* sailed handily down the strait, which opens up into Amundsen Gulf, then headed for the security of the harbour at Holman Island on the coast of Victoria Island. Larsen, his crew and the *St. Roch* had in effect traversed the Northwest Passage in the east-west direction, the first captain and ship ever to do so in one season. At the same time, Larsen became the first man to have sailed his ship through the Passage in both directions.

Anchored at Holman Island, Larsen received orders by short-wave radio from the commissioner of the RCMP to attempt completion of the trip that same year by reaching Vancouver before winter closed down navigation. The *St. Roch*'s trip home was far from over. There were still about 6,500 kilometres (4,000 miles) of sailing ahead of her before the sturdy little ship would finally slipped into her home port – and some of those kilometres would be as challenging as any of the trip. There was still the major problem, among others, of getting through the western Arctic ice pack before they could say they were completely safe from the crunching, jagged jaws of the floes. If the floes caught them, it could mean a whole extra year before getting home.

The *St. Roch* sailed out of the Holman Island harbour on September 5 and was almost immediately battling heavy ice. Ice and fog dogged Larsen and his ship for the next four days before they were able to anchor securely in the harbour at Tuktoyaktuk on the morning of September 9. Larsen tried to put out to sea again that same morning, but a heavy rainstorm with gale force winds convinced the captain to hunker down in a sheltered corner of the harbour to ride out the storm. And fortunate he was that he did. The gale turned into a hurricane that brought tremendous damage, flooding the Hudson's Bay Company buildings, washing away large quantities of trade goods and completely rearranging the geography of the harbour entrance. If the *St. Roch* had found herself at sea at the time, it is a virtual certainty that she would have been lost and, almost certainly, her men and women lost with her. It was not until September 17 that a change in wind and an improvement in weather encouraged Larsen to try leave Tuktoyaktuk through the mangled harbour entrance, which he did, but not without a grounding on the shallow bottom. A day later the *St. Roch*, to the accompaniment of ice and fog, reached the safety of the Herschel Island harbour.

On September 20, the wind and weather turned to the good, and Larsen took heart in the improved possibility of getting through the ice pack and reaching Vancouver that same year. There was no time to waste though, as the harbour was starting to ice over. The crew rapidly unloaded what supplies they had on board for Herschel Island and installed Panippakussuk, his wife, mother and the four children of his brother in one of the empty houses on shore, together with his seventeen dogs and eleven tons of coal. In the afternoon of September 21, 1944, the *St. Roch* and her crew said goodbye to the Inuit family. They lived at Herschel Island until the following year when Henry Larsen took them once again aboard the *St. Roch* to bring them east as far as Cambridge Bay from where they made it back to their eastern Arctic home on their own.

On September 24, the *St. Roch* steamed west in a narrow lead (an open channel in the ice) that hugged the shore of the mainland to port and skirted the edge of the ice pack to starboard. It became a race between the ship and the ice pack, which at this time of the year was tending to squeeze the lead closed, to lock itself solidly to the shoreline for the winter. If that happened before the *St. Roch* escaped, she would be immobilized in the ice pack until the following summer. Larsen's immediate objective was to reach Point Barrow as quickly as possible.

Beyond that point deep water prevailed and the ice pack would no longer be an enemy. He received a radio message from Barrow saying that the lead was closing. Larsen had no choice but to sail forward and race the ice since the lead was also closing behind him. The people of Barrow turned on all their lights to show Larsen where the shoreline was. It was music to his ears at 1:45 in the morning when he heard the man twirling the lead cry out, "We've lost the bottom!," meaning the ship had reached deep water and they were out of the ice's clutches. Barring any accidents, the *St. Roch* and her men would be spending Christmas ashore with their loved ones that year.

The sturdy little ship was now heading down the funnel leading to Bering Strait, which at the south end opens up into the Bering Sea. The weather in the Bering Sea was excellent and by October 1, the *St. Roch* entered Akutan harbour in the Aleutian Islands. Here they were able to refill their fuel and freshwater tanks. Larsen and his crew were treated royally to typical American hospitality with open messes, a movie and most important, the opportunity to take baths. The men luxuriated in this hospitality until October 4 when they set their compass on Unimak Pass leading into the North Pacific. By October 11, the expedition had reached the Queen Charlotte Islands where fog haunted it for the next five days, slowing it down until the morning of the 16th when the ship weighed anchor at ten o'clock and sailed all day in good weather, finally docking at Coleman Evans' wharf, Vancouver, at six o'clock in the afternoon of the same day, home at last.

The *St. Roch*, her captain and her men had set quite a record – they had completed a coast-to-coast trip through the Northwest Passage of some 11,750 kilometres (7,300 miles) in 86 days.

Although Roald Amundsen was the first ship's captain to sail his vessel through the Northwest Passage, he did so via a route that holds academic interest only, but no practical value for future commercial maritime navigation. The route taken by Amundsen in 1903–06 is, with minor deviations, the same as Larsen took in 1941–42. One thing that was amply proven by both those trips was that the route taken was too narrow and shoal-strewn to be of any use for commercial shipping. On the other hand, the route taken by Larsen in 1944 through Parry

Channel and Prince of Wales Strait will in all probability be the one that commercial shipping first uses when melting Arctic ice and favourable world market conditions make the proposition economically viable in not too many years.

CHAPTER FOURTEEN

Henry Larsen, The Sequel

IN 1945 LARSEN TOOK HIS NOW BELOVED *ST. ROCH* for their last Arctic wintering together. On the way back home through Bering Strait in 1946, he had a very strange and disturbing experience. A strong gale with minimal visibility forced the *St. Roch* to anchor for the night near an island without Larsen being absolutely certain of their exact position. When the fog finally lifted the following day, there was a Russian patrol boat anchored nearby. A motor launch carrying an armed boarding party was dispatched to investigate the *St. Roch*. It turned out that the little vessel had inadvertently strayed over the invisible line in the water between Russia and the United States. Larsen was removed from his ship and detained in a military station on shore until Moscow gave the word by radio the next day that he could rejoin his ship and be on his way. This he did posthaste and immediately made for Vancouver.

The following year, 1947, saw Larsen and the *St. Roch* leave Vancouver on their last Arctic patrol, anchoring at Herschel Island when freeze-up came. For the first time ever, Larsen left his ship iced-in for the winter and flew out to Vancouver to spend a month with his family[5] celebrating the Christmas holidays in Victoria. The Arctic was changing.

When the ship and her captain returned to dock in Vancouver on October 18, 1948, it was the end of a twenty-year Arctic love affair between a man and his ship. In the summer of 1950, the RCMP transferred the *St. Roch* from Vancouver through the Panama Canal to Halifax for duties in the eastern Arctic, thus becoming the first ship ever to circumnavigate the North American continent, going right around it, although not all in one continuous trip. Larsen would have loved to be her captain on this historic trip, but the RCMP deemed that his services were needed on land at Ottawa. The honour went to Officer Ken Hall instead

Although they never sailed together again in the Arctic, Larsen and his ship had one last fling in more southerly latitudes. After the *St. Roch* was returned to Halifax, it was decided that the stout little ship was no longer suited for RCMP patrol work and so she lay idle, tied to a Halifax dock for the next four years. In 1954, the good people of Vancouver insisted that Larsen be allowed to sail her west through the Panama Canal one last time to let her spend the rest of her days home where she belonged, in their city. The *St. Roch*'s arrival in Vancouver harbour was spectacular especially as it coincided closely with the arrival of another famous Canadian northern ship, the newly commissioned icebreaker *HMCS Labrador* under the command of Larsen's good friend, Captain Owen (Robbie) Robertson. The *St. Roch* was accorded the honour of leading the *Labrador* into Vancouver harbour in style, with the *Labrador*'s two helicopters hovering above. They were welcomed by the Navy Band and a large crowd of proud Vancouverites on the dock.

With the completion of the *St. Roch*'s last voyage, Larsen became the first captain ever to have circumnavigated the North American continent in the same vessel, although not in one sailing season. That latter honour belongs to Captain Robbie Robertson aboard HMCS *Labrador*. Robertson and his ship had left Halifax earlier in the year

St. Roch, flags flying, arriving in her final home in Vancouver in 1954. *Courtesy of Library and Archives Canada, E-003849452.*

and had traversed the Northwest Passage, meeting up with Larsen in Victoria and being escorted into Vancouver harbour by the *St. Roch*. Then he finally returned to his home port of Halifax through the Panama Canal, thus completing the circumnavigation.

The *St. Roch* was bought by the City of Vancouver for $5,000 and today sits proudly in a special building built for her at the Vancouver Maritime Museum.

During his post *St. Roch* years, Larsen moved up the ranks in the RCMP and finally retired on February 7, 1961 at the level of superintendent. In 1964, he made one last trip to his native Norway and on his return in September of that year he was so ill, he had to enter hospital where he died on October 29, 1964. He was 65 years of age.

PART THREE

Canadian Sovereignty and the Environment in the Northwest Passage Are at Risk

Westward from the Davis Strait 'tis there 'twas said to lie
The sea route to the Orient for which so many died;
Seeking gold and glory, leaving weathered, broken bones
And a long-forgotten lonely cairn of stones.[1]

– *Northwest Passage* – Stan Rogers

CHAPTER FIFTEEN

Canadian Sovereignty and the Environment in the Northwest Passage Are at Risk

THERE IS A LOT OF EVIDENCE SUPPORTING THE fact that Canada's northern regions are rapidly getting warmer and that Arctic ice is melting at a rate never before seen. In the fall of 2003, the University of Cambridge in the UK published the preliminary findings of the Arctic Climate Impact Assessment (ACIA) on Global Warming. The issue of Arctic warming is of particular concern to Canada because of its impact on its Arctic regions, including the Northwest Passage, and the potential it raises for threats to our northern environment and our sovereignty.

According to the ACIA's preliminary report, the "annual average arctic temperature has increased at almost twice the rate as that of the rest of the world over the past few decades."[2] The assessment foresees "additional arctic warming of about 4–7°C over the next 100 years." Four to seven degrees may not sound like a lot, but it is actually a huge increase in terms of the environmental changes that would result. Already, even with a seemingly minor increase in average Arctic

Disappearing ice threatens ability of polar bears to catch enough seals to survive.
Courtesy of the Canadian Coast Guard.

temperature in the last few decades, Arctic ice has thinned by an average of 10 to 15% according to the assessment.

It is not necessary for Arctic ice to completely disappear before the
Northwest Passage becomes effectively navigable by commercial traffic. As soon as it becomes economically practical for shipping lanes to
be kept open by icebreakers, ships will be lined up wanting to pass
through the long-sought trade route. The rising price of oil will also
hasten the day that ships start using the Passage for transporting
hydrocarbons since the economics of doing so will become more
favourable as oil prices rise.

The potentially negative environmental fallout through oil spills
and waste from passing ships is frightening to contemplate. At risk are
the Inuit, their marine and terrestrial food animals – whales, seals wal-
ruses, polar bears, fish – and plants. It is important that Canada face
the eventuality of an open Passage as soon as possible before the maritime traffic through it starts in earnest. Measures must be put in place
to enable our country to adequately monitor, control, service, assist
and rescue, when required, the expected traffic, and to mitigate the
potentially disastrous impact of this traffic on our environment.

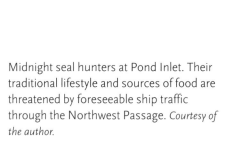

Midnight seal hunters at Pond Inlet. Their traditional lifestyle and sources of food are threatened by foreseeable ship traffic through the Northwest Passage. *Courtesy of the author.*

A crucial part of this environmental issue is the question of whether or not the Northwest Passage constitutes *our* environment; Canadian sovereignty over the waters of the Northwest Passage is not a foregone conclusion at this time. It has been assailed in the past, and indeed recently, in particular by the United States. In order to effectively carry out the above mentioned responsibilities in the Passage, it is essential that Canada be able to demonstrate to the world that she is sovereign over the waters of the Passage, and to do so not only with words, but also by building the human and material infrastructure necessary for discharging those responsibilities. Without solidly proven sovereignty, Canada would be severely limited in its capability to put into place, and enforce, measures essential for the protection of the environment in the Passage from the potential negative impact of maritime shipping.

The following pages explore the intimately related issues of sovereignty and health of the environment in the Northwest Passage.

CHAPTER SIXTEEN

United Nations Convention on the Law of the Sea (UNCLOS)

IN 1982, THE UNITED NATIONS PROMULGATED the United Nations Convention on the Law of the Sea. In 1994, UNCLOS became international law. Some 150 countries have ratified the convention, including Canada, but the United States has not.

The convention sets down, among other things, a detailed set of laws governing the nations of the world with respect to the rights and responsibilities of coastal nations in three bands of sea off the coast of those nations, including the air above the bands, as well as the water and the seabed beneath. The bands measure 12, 24 and 200 nautical miles.[3] These are bands of varying degrees of sovereignty attributed to nations with a seacoast. UNCLOS also sets down the rights and responsibilities of countries, coastal or not, that will send their ships to navigate those coastal waters. There do not appear to be major issues of disagreement concerning this part of UNCLOS with respect to the Northwest Passage. The part of the convention that rankles the United States is the one that says a country with an archipelago of islands, can,

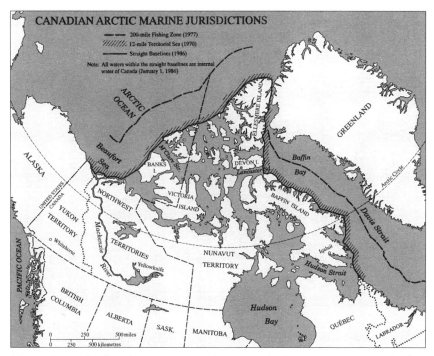

Map outlining the Canadian marine jurisdictions in the Arctic, Note in particular the "straight baselines" of 1986 surrounding the Arctic Archipelago. Taken from Gordon Robertson, *Memoirs of a Very Civil Servant*, 105.

by drawing straight baselines from headland to headland, surround the whole archipelago and join it to the mainland of the coastal country as an entity. This effectively makes all the inter-island, and archipelago-to-mainland straits of water, internal waters of that country. Canada took this step of defining the straight baselines for its Arctic Archipelago in 1986.

Accordingly, Canada claims that she enjoys complete sovereignty over those waters as internal waters, which means that she can, in law, deny the right of passage to foreign ships through those waters – not that Canada would necessarily want to do that. However, transiting ships would be governed by whatever regulations Canada saw fit to enact, in order to safeguard its sovereignty and environment.

However, U.S. Ambassador David Wilkins doesn't see things the same way. On January 22, 2006, he was quoted in the media as saying regarding Canadian Arctic waters, "We don't recognize Canada's claims to those waters. Most other countries do not recognize their claims." His statement is dead wrong. As noted above, since 1982 the UN convention known as the United Nations Convention on the Law of the Sea has been in existence. Canada's claim of sovereignty in the Arctic rests on the fact that in 1986, she fulfilled all the requirements of UNCLOS to establish her claim. This includes the publication of what are called straight baselines, which enclose Canada's Arctic Archipelago and tie it to the mainland. All waters within the area defined, including the Northwest Passage, are internal waters of Canada according to the convention's provisions. Of the world's 190 or so countries, approximately 150 have ratified UNCLOS and are bound by its provisions. Among these countries are the European Community countries, the UK, Russia, Japan, China, Norway, Sweden, Finland, Denmark, Iceland and Canada – but not the United States. Landlocked Switzerland is the only major international player that has not ratified UNCLOS, with good reason – it has no coastline.

The United States finds itself on the outside with some 40 other, minor countries that for various internal reasons have not ratified the convention. Approximately half of them are landlocked and so have no more reason to ratify the convention than Switzerland. The United States, thus, finds itself alone on this issue, in the company of a group of twenty or so other non-ratifiers that does not represent a huge amount of presence on the international scene. Wilkins was also wrong when he stated that, "Most other countries do not recognize their [Canada's] claims." One hundred-and-fifty countries have ratified UNCLOS. Prime Minister Stephen Harper was right to rebuke him. Canada has fulfilled all the requirements of UNCLOS for claiming internal waters.

In 1935, Norway was the first country to define a part of its coastline by drawing straight baselines from headland to headland across indentations and mouths of fiords and to refuse foreign ships the right to enter their fiords and other indentations without permission. Their actions were contested by Great Britain in 1951 before the International Court of Justice (IJC), which ruled that Norway was within its rights to draw such lines. The following year, Norway drew straight baselines along the entirety of its coastline from the border with Russia in the north to its border with Sweden to the south. Much of the language and concepts of the ICJ's 1951 decision favouring Norway have found their way into Article 7 of UNCLOS.[4]

It is high time the United States joined the great majority of the world's countries, including all the major ones, in recognizing UNCLOS, a UN convention that expresses the interests of the countries of the world as a whole, rather than the interest of any one country. Furthermore, Canada's position has always been that she considers the waters in question to be her internal waters, and therefore subject to her sovereignty. As well, the waters of the Northwest Passage have never been declared international waters. Canada's position was made clear in 1973 by the legal bureau of the Department of External Affairs:

> Canada ... claims that the waters of the Canadian Arctic Archipelago are internal waters of Canada on an historical basis.[5]

In 1975, then Secretary of State for External Affairs Allan MacEachen reiterated the claim when he appeared before the Standing Committee for External Affairs and National Defence:

> As Canada's Northwest Passage is not used for international navigation and since Arctic Waters are considered by Canada as being internal waters, the regime of transit passage does not apply to the Arctic.[6]

Donat Pharand, an internationally renowned Canadian expert on maritime law, has demonstrated in his books on the legal aspects of the Northwest Passage that there are longstanding precedents strongly supporting the legal opinion that these waters do not meet the characteristics required for them to be considered to be international waters. These characteristics include, for example, "the number of ships passing through, their total tonnage, the aggregate value of their cargoes,

The *Manhattan* sailing through the Northwest Passage, without having sought permission in 1969. *Courtesy of the Canadian Coast Guard.*

the average size of the ships, and especially whether they are distrib-
uted among a greater or smaller number of nations"[7] It is quite evident
that these characteristics are insignificant with respect to the minis-
cule amount of traffic through the passage. The Northwest Passage
today is not, and never has been an international strait.

Despite Canada's legitimate claims, the U.S. position has been, and
still is, that it considers those waters to be international waters, and that
they are subject to the laws regarding international navigation, which
translates into having the right to pass without asking permission. That
the Americans are dead serious about denying Canadian sovereignty
over the Northwest Passage waters was concretely expressed in 1969.
That year the Americans sent the 150,000 ton *Manhattan* through the
Passage without asking permission of Canada, although Canada collaborated in the transit by having a Canadian representative on board.
Also, one of her icebreakers assisted the huge tanker in navigating the
ice fields. In 1985, the United States again sent a ship through the
Passage without asking permission when their icebreaker *Polar Sea*
made the transit. In this case, Canada protested with the result that the
United States and Canada agreed to disagree on the issue. There have
now been many U.S. violations of Canadian sovereignty in Arctic
waters over the years. The battle lines are clearly drawn.

CHAPTER SEVENTEEN

Sovereignty Is What Sovereignty Does

PERHAPS THE MOST COMPELLING REASONS WHY
Canada must not delay getting ready for a Northwest Passage open to
navigation is to ensure the integrity of her land and waters, to ensure
their sovereignty and protect their environment. If the United States
continues to violate the sovereignty of Canadian waters, this would
compromise our capability to protect the shores of our Arctic mainland to the south of the Passage, and the shores of our Arctic islands to
the north, from potentially negative environmental effects of shipping.

The issue for Canada boils down to being able to demonstrate that
the waters of the various channels of the Northwest Passage have
always been subject to Canadian sovereignty, at least since Britain
ceded her northern domain to Canada in 1880, and will continue to be
so, in the future. Prior to 1880, the navigators of our Arctic waters were
almost exclusively British. While there were some Americans who
went up North, such as Peary and Greely, they did nothing to compromise our sovereignty or establish theirs.

The bird covered in an oily residue is an example of irresponsible shipping activities that impact negatively on the environment and on traditional food sources. *Courtesy of Environment Canada.*

In that respect, it would be useful that a Canadian project be established with the purpose of mining Arctic history to gather all the pertinent nuggets, both from written history and from oral, particularly Inuit history. Such research would lead to weaving the findings into a written tapestry with the express purpose of demonstrating the sovereign role played by the British Empire and Canada for many decades in the land and waters of the Arctic. It is necessary to build such a case if, and before, the International Court of Justice is called upon to adjudicate the issue of sovereignty over the waters of the Northwest Passage.

With respect to the present and especially the future of the Northwest Passage, there is much still to be done. It is one thing to *claim* sovereignty over Arctic lands and waters. It is quite another thing to *demonstrate* sovereignty in a solid, concrete and unassailable way by significant and meaningful Canadian activities in the Arctic. But there is also another compelling reason, in addition to sovereignty, for Canada to become more active than it is at present in the Arctic. It is a business reason.

Assuredly, sooner or later, the Northwest Passage will become one of the world's more important ocean shipping routes. Even at this time, in 2006, sailing through the Northwest Passage is technologically feasible at any time of the year with an Polar Class 8 icebreaker or icebreaking tanker. It would be expensive to do so, but it is doable. The reason the Northwest Passage has not yet become an established shipping route is not one of technology, but rather one of economics. There are still cheaper ways of transporting Arctic goods, for example Arctic oil and gas by pipelines. But that can change at any time. Oil and gas companies already have fully developed plans to use ice-breaking tankers for transporting hydrocarbons through the Passage. All it would take to tip the scale in that direction is an oil crisis in the Middle East that restricted availability and caused a sharp increase in fuel prices. Couple that with global warming and its thinning effect on Arctic ice, and the economics for shipping hydrocarbons through the Northwest Passage could quickly become favourable. If the Canadian government is not well prepared for that day in terms of being able to adequately monitor, control, service and assist shipping through the Passage, she could end up standing in the way of private enterprise. Canada will one day be subjected to increasing international pressure to allow shipping via these waters. The day may not be that far off. It could be prejudicial for business if Canada did not have a proper maritime traffic surveillance, control and assistance system in operation, as well as the ability to provide the other services that transiting ships will need. If she could not provide these services, Canada would be hard pressed to claim sovereignty over the waters of the Northwest Passage. What, then. must Canada do to protect her sovereignty and prepare herself for the era of major Maritime traffic through the passage?

In 1985, the government of the day appeared to have a good handle on what had to be done to protect Canada's sovereignty over the Arctic and particularly, the Northwest Passage. On September 10 of that year, Secretary of State for External Affairs, the Right Honourable Joe Clark rose in the House of Commons and made a statement on the issue that contained the following words, excerpt as recorded in Hansard:

> Mr. Speaker
> Sovereignty can arouse deep emotion in this country.
> That is to be expected for sovereignty speaks to the very
> identity and character of a people. We Canadians want
> to be ourselves. We want to control our own affairs and
> take charge of our own destiny. At the same time, we

want to look beyond ourselves and to play a constructive part in a world community that grows more
independent every year. We have something to offer
and something to gain in so doing.

In domestic policy, in foreign policy, and in
defence policy, this government has given Canadian
sovereignty a new impetus within a new maturity. But
much remains to be done. The voyage of the Polar Sea
[an American icebreaker, August, 1985] demonstrated
that Canada, in the past, had not developed the means
to ensure our sovereignty over time. During that
voyage, Canada's legal claim was fully protected, but
when we looked for tangible ways to exercise our sovereignty, we found that our cupboard was nearly bare.

Mr. Speaker
The implications for Canada are clear. As the Western
country with by far the greatest frontage on the Arctic,
we must come up to speed in a range of marine operations that bear on our capacity to exercise effective
control over the Northwest Passage and our other Arctic
waters.

Canada is an Arctic nation. The international community has long recognized that the Arctic Mainland
and islands are a part of Canada like any other. But the
Arctic is not only a part of Canada. It is part of Canada's
greatness.

The policy of this government is to preserve that
greatness undiminished.

In summary, Mr. Speaker, these are the measures that
we are announcing today:

1. immediate adoption of an order in council establishing straight baselines around the Arctic archipelago, to be effective January 1, 1986;

2. immediate adoption of a Canadian Laws Offshore Application Act;

3. immediate talks with the United States on cooperation in Arctic waters, on the basis of full respect for Canadian sovereignty;

4. an immediate increase of surveillance overflights of our Arctic waters by aircraft of the Canadian forces, and immediate planning for Canadian naval activity in the Eastern Arctic in 1986;

5. the immediate withdrawal of the 1970 reservation to Canada's acceptance of the compulsory jurisdiction of the International Court of Justice; and

6. construction of a Polar Class 8 icebreaker and urgent consideration of other means of exercising more effective control over our Arctic waters.

These are the measures we can take immediately. We know, however, that a long-term commitment is required. We are making that commitment today.[8]

The American icebreaker *Polar Sea* violated Canada's sovereignty in the Arctic in August 1985; the Canadian government made its position clear in Joe Clark's statement less than a month later on September 10, 1985; straight baselines around the Arctic Archipelago were officially established on January 1, 1986. This is unusually quick action for a government. The issue was no doubt considered of extreme importance. What happened next? What happened to the long-term commitment promised in the statement?

The issue of straight baselines was undoubtedly the most crucial one. That action clearly established Canada's position. It was an action that was necessary and it did not cost any significant expenditure of funds. Nor did the implementation of measures two, three, four and five. When it came to the half-a-billion dollar Polar Class 8 icebreaker, however, that is a different story. It was never built. Thus ended the long-term government commitment.

The American ice-breaker, *Polar Sea*, another visitor to Canadian waters sailing through the Passage without asking permission. *Courtesy of the Canadian Coast Guard.*

Canada is clearly not ready today for maritime traffic through the Passage with respect to enforcing her sovereignty. This was demon-strated in spades by the Hans Island incident of the late summer and early fall of 2005. Hans Island is an insignificant piece of rock sticking out in the high Arctic strait that separates Canada's Ellesmere Island and Denmark's Greenland. Insignificant – except for the fact that there is oil beneath it and the island could be very useful as a drilling platform. The problem with Hans Island is it appears that the international boundary line between Canada and Denmark splits it in two. In August 2005, Denmark made moves to send a naval expedition to the island claiming that the island was entirely hers. Canada protested saying half of it was Canadian. There followed a "my-father-is-stronger-than-your-father type" of standoff until cooler heads prevailed and the two countries more or less agreed to disagree. The worrisome (for Canada) fact the standoff revealed was that Denmark was better prepared than Canada to protect their sovereignty over Hans Island, or at least their part of the island. Little Denmark has at least one naval vessel that it can dispatch to the region of the island. Canada does not have even one naval vessel that is ice-capable for working in that part of the Arctic.

Without a doubt, sovereignty issues that Canada has with the United States, and with Denmark, must be addressed at a legal/politi-cal/diplomatic level even as we gird ourselves with the technological wherewithal to properly manage a Northwest Passage that will open to maritime traffic sooner than we think. It is obviously not realistic to think that Canada could ever stand down the United States in the Northwest Passage on a basis of military might. This is not to say that Canada will not need some military capability to face unforeseen potential situations that could require it. However, more urgent at this time is to address the U.S./Denmark issue at a diplomatic level while we plan for all the duties Canada will have to discharge with respect to ships passing through her Arctic waters.

Canadian Professor of Law, Donat Pharand, in his book *The Northwest Passage: Arctic Straits,* writes of "Technological Sovereignty," referring to the technological infrastructure that Canada must have to effectively protect her sovereignty in Arctic waters. Achieving technological sovereignty would require that Canada have today, or would have in place in the near future, the technology needed to protect her sovereignty over the Passage through her capacity to ensure the safe and efficient operation and control of shipping through the Passage, including the provision of all the services that will be required by the transiting ships. This is far from being the case at present.

In 1982, at meetings of the Beaufort Sea Environment Assessment Panel, the Department of Transport indicated that it should be in a position to provide the following services to shipping using the Northwest Passage: "Marine navigational aids, icebreaking and escorting, marine search and rescue, marine emergencies/pollution control, marine mobile communications services, ports, harbours and terminals, vessel inspection services, vessel traffic management, marine re-supply administration and support, pilotage and training." Transport also offered the following services to be supplied by other departments of government: "hydrography, oceanography, ice properties, ice distribution and movements, meteorology, dredging implementation and customs services."[9]

Today, in 2006, twenty-three years later, it is obvious that a significant number of these essential services are still not available, nor, it appears, will they be for some time to come. Long intervals are required to be able to provide them. For example, Canada doesn't have icebreakers,

The *Louis St. Laurent*, Canada's largest icebreaker, is not strong enough for full Arctic service year around. *Courtesy of the Canadian Coast Guard.*

nor are any planned, of sufficient strength to service the class of ships that will be used for transporting hydrocarbons. Canada's two heaviest-duty icebreakers, the *Louis S. St-Laurent* and the *Terry Fox*, are the approximate equivalent of Arctic Class 6 icebreakers (for some internal reason Canadian Coast Guard icebreakers are not assigned an Arctic Class). Oil and gas tankers of Arctic classes 8 and 10 are foreseen for this traffic. However, at this time the Canadian government has no plans to acquire Polar Class 8 icebreakers (the equivalent to Arctic classes 8 and 10 oil and gas tankers) to provide assistance to ships in case of need. It takes a long time to acquire such icebreakers and they do not come cheap. The estimated cost twenty years ago was $500 million each. The cost in 2006 would no doubt be higher, quite a bit higher especially if they are to carry troops and be armed as Prime Minister Harper has proposed. Yet, heavy-duty icebreakers are a *sine qua non* for being able to properly exercise sovereignty over the waters of the Passage.[10]

Where are the helicopters in numbers and types adequate for effective search and rescue in the Arctic when it becomes host to heavy ship traffic? Where are the submarines and undersea detection systems for monitoring and controlling undersea traffic, either authorized or unauthorized? There is good evidence that foreign submarines are cruising under Canadian waters today without Canada necessarily being aware if it. There is a vessel monitoring and advisory system in place called NORDREG, but compliance with NORDREG is voluntary and relies highly on the competence of the ice masters aboard transiting ships to ensure safe navigation practices. It should be compulsory, not voluntary.

An issue of great importance is the development of adequate Disaster Mitigation Plans For the Northwest Passage. Put simply, these plans consist of a series of *What if?* questions, and fully developed answers. For example:

1. What if there is an oil spill? Potential answer: The equipment to handle oil spills is stored in locations X, Y & Z; the following are the people who are responsible for acting; here are their responsibilities; here are the people/organizations to notify; and many more items.
2. What if there is a fire aboard a ship?
3. What if a tanker sinks in the shipping lane and blocks it?
4. What if there is a collision? What if there are many injured people?
5. What if a big passenger ship gets stuck? (The latter has already happened. In 1998 the German cruise ship *Hanseatic* ran aground in the waters immediately south of King William Island and some 150 passengers had to be evacuated to Cambridge Bay.)
6. What if a serious medical emergency occurs on a large cruise ship including a breakout of disease or food poisoning, and so on.

It is essential that mitigation plans be developed to cope with the full range of potentially devastating disasters under the exacting conditions that prevail in the Northwest Passage.

It is quite likely that Canada, on her own, will find it very difficult to come up with the financial resources required to satisfy the need for marine services that an open Northwest Passage will generate. Nor should she be expected to. These services will eventually be mainly for the benefit of ships of foreign countries wishing to take advantage of the shorter shipping route and they should pay for these services. But how will they pay? It is not realistic to think that Canada alone would provide the capital resources up front to create all the required services, to only recover costs over time through user fees. The initial amount required will be staggering and too great for Canada to support alone. A suggested way to attack this problem is the following: An organization called, let us say, the International Commission for the Northwest Passage (or some such name), should be formed, grouping Canada and at least the seven other circumpolar countries as well as pertinent private sector representatives. A major purpose of the organization would be to develop schemes for equitable sharing of responsibilities with respect to an open Northwest Passage such as, among other things, raising capital for the implementation of the infrastructure required to permit safe and efficient use, control and monitoring of the Northwest Passage for the benefit of Canada and prospective other user countries. Because of Canada's claim to sovereignty over the waters of the Passage and the fact that she has an almost exclusive share of the environmental vulnerability due to maritime traffic in the Passage, she must have a predominant voice and role in such a Commission.

An example of international collaboration is the case of the Northeast Passage north of Russia. Three interested countries – Russia, Norway and Japan – collaborated on a study for the planning, implementation and management of a shipping corridor through the Northern Sea Route, as it is called. The study took five years and yielded a stack of research documentation well over a metre in height. Japan was the major financial supporter of the study. Such collaborative initiatives should be explored for the Northwest Passage.

Timing is critical. But time is not on the Canadian government's side. The private sector can swing into action and be ready to commence shipping operations through the Passage much more quickly than it will take Canada to settle its international legal/political/diplomatic issues of sovereignty on the one hand, and to implement the required physical/human infrastructure, on the other. Both those items will take many years to settle and implement. There is a lot of inertia to overcome in our bureaucracy-bound government processes. Several petroleum companies already have fully developed plans for shipping hydrocarbons through the Passage. Should the economic landscape become favourable, ships may relatively quickly start navigating the Passage before adequate surveillance, control systems, or disaster mitigation plans are in place, risking potentially devastating environmental consequences. The longer Canada waits before acting, the shorter becomes the already too short lead-time at her disposal to take action. Playing a waiting game risks forcing our country into an undesirable panic situation. What is the alternative?

Franklyn Griffiths in his introduction to the book he edited in 1986, *Politics of the Northwest Passage*, put forth a bold and interesting concept – "Making It Happen." Instead of merely *letting* things happen to us in the Northwest Passage on someone else's terms, Griffiths proposed that Canada take the bull by the horns and lead a viable, collaborative effort to *direct* what happens in the Arctic, on Canada's own terms. "Making It Happen" is a forward-looking approach requiring visionary thinking.

In the early 1970s, Canada had a healthy northern vision that thrust the country into the forefront of technical progress in the north. She had the foresight to realize that a major key to the development of the north, and particularly its people, was telecommunications. In 1972, Telesat Canada launched the world's first domestic, geostationary, telecommunications satellite called ANIK – meaning brother in Inuktitut. There had been heated debates in Parliament and the project did not pass without difficulties. The main reason for the difficulties was that no one could prove, based on dollar figures, that the project would be economically sound, that it would be profitable. The technology was not yet mature, and the market that would exist for the services the satellite would stimulate was anybody's guess. However, economic faintheartedness did not carry the day. What convinced the Houses of Parliament to approve the project, and to move ahead with it, was a forward-looking vision that saw a satellite telecommunications system being of great value in the long run for the development of the North, and especially its people – by breaking their fetters of isolation. ANIK was not sold by proving that it would be economically sound. It could not be proven that way at the time. Instead, Canada made an educated guess with the information at hand that telecommunications would be of great value for the development of the North, its people and the country as a whole. Many millions were spent to launch the Anik system and many more millions were added later on to expand it. Was the educated guess correct? The answer is history. Modern telecommunications have proven to be a tremendous impetus to the development of the North and especially her people. The vision has proven sound in all respects, including economic.

Canada is in a similar position today with respect to the Northwest Passage. The stakes are higher, but the basic situation is much the same. Is there any doubt that as the Northwest Passage becomes more easily navigable, there will be a steadily growing number of international industries that will want to ship their products through it? There is no doubt that heavy ship traffic will generate significant business opportunities for Canadian enterprises. Not only for mineral extraction industries, but also for industries that will be needed to service the heavy traffic; not only of passing vessels and people, but also of the increasing number of vessels and people that will have a destination, long or short term, *in* the Arctic. There is no doubt that user fees are capable of generating significant revenue. For the year 2002, the Panama Canal Authority had a budgetary item of the equivalent of one billion Canadian dollars in revenue from user fees.

It is not a question of "if" maritime traffic starts using the Northwest Passage, but one of "when." Indications are that the "when" may be upon us sooner than we think. What is needed at this point is a change of mindset from one that looks upon ship traffic through the Northwest

Passage as a problem to be dreaded, and to replace it with one that sees the situation as an opportunity for development of the North, its people and the country as a whole. The traffic should be welcomed. It will come in any case, along with business opportunities for local populations – better to prepare and be ready for it, and to take advantage of it, than to have it take advantage of us. It is time to be proactive with respect to the Northwest Passage.

CHAPTER EIGHTEEN

Attacking the Issues

SEVERAL MINISTRIES OF THE CANADIAN
government will be affected by a Northwest Passage open to commer-
cial maritime traffic. Following is a list of the principal pertinent ones:
Environment Canada, Finance Canada, Fisheries and Oceans Canada,
Foreign Affairs & International Trade Canada, Indian and Northern
Affairs Canada, Industry Canada, Justice Canada, National Defence
Canada, Natural Resources Canada and Transport Canada.

It is urgent that a government body, let us call it the Canadian
Northwest Passage Commission (CNWPC), be formed without delay,
composed of an appropriate Assistant Deputy Minister from each
Ministry, to spearhead an initiative, the purpose of which would be to
ensure the preparedness of Canada to cope effectively, and in a timely
fashion, with the foreseeable opening of the Northwest Passage to
international and domestic marine traffic. It is further suggested that
Foreign Affairs and International Trade Canada, together with
Transport Canada, chair the Commission jointly.

The proposed CNWPC should be tasked with the creation of a Master Fundamental Plan for the development of the Canadian Northwest Passage (CNWP) on an economically, environmentally, socially and militarily sound basis. It is further suggested that the Commission be tasked with identifying all the issues that are to be considered with respect to the future of the CNWP and to initiate studies to address these issues in depth. A suggested non-inclusive list of issues to be addressed in a Master Fundamental Plan is included in Appendix II.

The price of inactivity is considerable. The price of not acting at this stage could well mean the eventual division of our precious country into Canada North and Canada South, with a channel of international waters running between mainland Canada and her Arctic Archipelago, waters over which she would not exercise sovereignty. Add to that price the loss of effective control over potentially negative environmental impacts that could result from international shipping operations, and particularly from oil and gas tankers, transiting through the Passage. And add to that again, the loss of Canada's right to control, and if necessary, to prevent any ship from passing through the Northwest Passage if the vessel is *not* in so-called "Innocent Passage." (Innocent Passage simply means that the ship intends us no harm and otherwise respects the international laws of Innocent Passage.)

To not act now could well provoke a catastrophe of monumental proportions for which future generations of Canadians could rightly reproach the present generation.

This must not be allowed to happen.

Appendix I

Statement in the House of Commons by the Secretary of State for External Affairs, the Right Honourable Joe Clark, on Canadian Sovereignty (September 10, 1985).

Mr. Speaker,

Sovereignty can arouse deep emotion in this country. That is to be expected, for sovereignty speaks to the very identity and character of a people. We Canadians want to be ourselves. We want to control our own affairs and take charge of our own destiny. At the same time, we want to look beyond ourselves and to play a constructive part in a world community that grows more interdependent every year. We have something to offer and something to gain in so doing.

The sovereignty question has concerned this government since we were first sworn in. We have built national unity, we have strengthened the national economy, because unity and strength are hallmarks of sovereignty as they are hallmarks of this government's policy and achievements.

In unity and strength, we have taken action to increase Canadian ownership of the Canadian petroleum industry. We have declared a Canadian ownership policy in respect of foreign investment in the publishing industry. We have made our own Canadian decisions on controversial issues of foreign policy – such as Nicaragua and South Africa. We have passed the *Foreign Extraterritorial Measures Act* to block unacceptable claims of jurisdiction by foreign governments or courts seeking to extend their writ to Canada. We have arrested foreign trawlers poaching in our fishing zones. We have taken important steps to improve Canada's defences notably in bolstering Canadian forces in Europe and in putting into place a new North Warning System to protect Canadian sovereignty over our northern airspace.

And we have reconstructed relations with traditional friends and allies, who have welcomed our renewed unity and strength and the confidence they generate.

In domestic policy, in foreign policy, and in defence policy, this government has given Canadian sovereignty a new impetus within a new maturity. But much remains to be done. The voyage of the *Polar Sea* demonstrated that Canada, in the past, had not developed the means to ensure our sovereignty over time. During that voyage, Canada's legal claim was fully protected, but when we looked for tangible ways to exercise our sovereignty, we found that our cupboard was nearly bare. We obtained from the United States a formal and explicit assurance that the voyage of the *Polar Sea* was without prejudice to Canada's legal position. That is an assurance, which the government of the day, in 1969, did not receive for the voyage of the *Manhattan* and of the two United States Coast Guard icebreakers. For the future, non-prejudicial arrangements will not be enough.

The voyage of the *Polar Sea* has left no trace on Canada's Arctic waters and no mark on Canada's Arctic sovereignty. It is behind us, and our concern must be with what lies ahead.

Many countries, including the United States and the Federal Republic of Germany, are actively preparing for commercial navigation in Arctic waters. Developments are accelerating in ice science, ice technology, and tanker design. Several major Japanese firms are moving to capture the market for icebreaking tankers once polar oil and gas come on stream. Soviet submarines are being deployed under the Arctic ice pack, and the United States Navy in turn has identified a need to gain Arctic operational experience to counter new Soviet deployments.

Mr. Speaker

The implications for Canada are clear. As the Western country with by far the greatest frontage on the Arctic, we must come up to speed in a range of marine operations that bear on our capacity to exercise effective control over the Northwest Passage and our other Arctic waters.

To this end, I wish to declare to the House the policy of this government in respect of Canadian sovereignty in Arctic waters, and to make a number of announcements as to how we propose to give expression to that policy.

Canada is an Arctic nation. The international community has long recognized that the Arctic mainland and islands are a part of Canada like any other. But the Arctic is not only a part of Canada. It is part of Canada's greatness.

The policy of this government is to preserve that greatness undiminished. Canada's sovereignty in the Arctic is indivisible. It embraces land, sea, and ice. It extends without interruption to the seaward-facing coasts of the Arctic islands. These islands are joined and not divided by the waters between them. They are bridged for most of the year by ice. From time immemorial Canada's Inuit people have used and occupied the ice as they have used and occupied the land.

The policy of this government is to maintain the natural unity of the Canadian Arctic Archipelago, and to preserve Canada's sovereignty over land, sea, and ice undiminished and undivided.

That sovereignty has long been upheld by Canada. No previous government, however, has defined its precise limits or delineated Canada's internal waters and territorial sea in the Arctic. This government proposes to do so. An order in council establishing straight baselines around the outer perimeter of the Canadian Arctic Archipelago has been signed today, and will come into effect on January 1, 1986. These baselines define the outer limit of Canada's historic internal waters. Canada's territorial waters extend 12 miles seaward of the baselines. While the *Territorial Sea and Fishing Zones Act* requires 60 days' notice only for the establishment of fisheries limits, we consider that prior notice should also be given for this important step of establishing straight baselines.

Canada enjoys the same undisputed jurisdiction over its continental margin and 200-mile fishing zone in the Arctic as elsewhere. To protect the unique ecological balance of the region, Canada also exercises jurisdiction over a 200-mile pollution prevention zone in the Arctic waters. This too has been recognized by the international community, through a special provision in the United Nations Convention on the Law of the Sea.

No previous government, however, has extended the application of Canadian civil and criminal law to offshore areas, in the Arctic and elsewhere. This government will do so. To this end, we shall give priority to the early adoption of a *Canadian Laws Offshore Application Act.*

The exercise of functional jurisdiction in Arctic waters is essential to Canadian interests. But it can never serve as a substitute for the exercise of Canada's full sovereignty over the waters of the Arctic archipelago. Only full sovereignty protects the full range of Canada's interests. This full sovereignty is vital to Canada's security. It is vital to Canada's Inuit people. And it is vital even to Canada's nationhood.

The policy of this government is to exercise Canada's full sovereignty in and over the waters of the Arctic Archipelago. We will accept no substitutes.

The policy of this government is also to encourage the development of navigation in Canada's Arctic waters. Our goal is to make the Northwest Passage a reality for Canadian and foreign shipping, as a Canadian waterway. Navigation, however, will be subject to the controls and other measures required for Canada's security, for the preservation of the environment, and for the welfare of the Inuit and other inhabitants of the Canadian Arctic.

In due course, the government will announce the further steps it is taking to implement these policies, and especially to provide more extensive marine support services, to strengthen regulatory structures, and to reinforce the necessary means of control. I am announcing today that the government has decided to construct a Polar Class 8 icebreaker. The Ministers of National Defence and Transport will shortly bring to Cabinet recommendations with regard to design and construction plans. The costs are very high, in the order of half a billion dollars. But this government is not about to conclude that Canada cannot afford the Arctic. Meanwhile, we are taking immediate steps to increase surveillance overflights of our Arctic waters by Canadian Forces aircraft. In addition, we are now making plans for naval activity in eastern Arctic waters in 1986.

Canada is a strong and responsible member of the international community. Our strength and our responsibility make us all the more aware of the need for cooperation with other countries, and especially with our friends and allies. Cooperation is necessary not only in defence to our own interests but in defence of the common interests of the international community. Cooperation adds to our strength and in no way diminishes our sovereignty.

The policy of this government is to offer its cooperation to its friends and allies, and to seek their cooperation in return.

We are prepared to explore with the United States all means of cooperation that might promote the respective interests of both countries, as Arctic friends, neighbours, and allies, in the Arctic waters of Canada and Alaska. The United States has been made aware that Canada wishes to open talks on this matter in the near future. Any cooperation with the United States, or with other Arctic nations, shall only be on the basis of full respect for Canada's sovereignty. That too has been made clear.

In 1970, the government of the day barred the International Court of Justice from hearing disputes that might arise concerning the jurisdiction exercised by Canada for the prevention of pollution in Arctic waters.

This government will remove that bar Indeed, we have today notified the Secretary General of the United Nations that Canada is withdrawing the 1970 reservation to its acceptance of the compulsory jurisdiction of the World Court.

The Arctic is a heritage for the people of Canada. They are determined to keep their heritage entire.

The policy of this government is to give full expression to that determination.

We challenge no established rights, for none have been established except by Canada. We set no precedent for other areas, for no other area compares with the Canadian Arctic Archipelago. We are confident in our position. We believe in the rule of law in international relations. We shall act in accordance with our confidence and belief, as we are doing today in withdrawing the 1970 reservation to Canada's acceptance of the compulsory jurisdiction of the World Court. We are prepared to uphold our position in that Court, if necessary, and to have it freely and fully judged there.

In summary, Mr. Speaker, these are the measures we are announcing today:

1. immediate adoption of an order in council establishing straight baselines around the Arctic archipelago, to be effective January 1, 1986;
2. immediate adoption of a *Canadian Laws Offshore Application Act;*
3. immediate talks with the United States on cooperation in Arctic waters, on the basis of full respect for Canadian sovereignty;
4. an immediate increase of surveillance overflights of our Arctic waters by aircraft of the Canadian Forces, and immediate planning for Canadian naval activity in the Eastern Arctic in 1986;
5. the immediate withdrawal of the 1970 reservation to Canada's acceptance of the compulsory jurisdiction of the International Court of Justice; and
6. construction of a Polar Class 8 icebreaker and urgent consideration of other means of exercising more effective control over our Arctic Waters.

These are the measures we can take immediately. We know, however, that a long-term commitment is required. We are making that commitment today.

Appendix II

Suggested Non-Inclusive List of Issues to Be Addressed in a Master Fundamental Plan under the proposed Canadian Northwest Passage Commission (CNWPC).

1 – Creation of a history of the exercise of sovereignty in the Arctic – pre-1880 by the British and post-1880 by Canadians – in preparation for the eventuality of having to appear before the International Court of Justice;

2 – Development of an ironclad legal case for Canadian Arctic sovereignty for presentation to the International Court of Justice at the appropriate time, if and when required;

3 – Development of various possible scenarios of timing for the beginning of commercial maritime traffic operations in the CNWP* and projections of its subsequent growth in the ensuing years;

4 – Development of a plan, for each scenario, for implementation of adequate surveillance, monitoring, control of, and assistance to, the foreseen traffic over a reasonable period of years;

5 – Development of a plan for the procurement of a fleet of aircraft, and particularly helicopters, required for adequate surveillance, monitoring, control of, and assistance to, surface and undersea craft operating in the CNWP;

6 – Development of a plan for the procurement of a fleet of aircraft for military and transportation duties relating to enforcement;

7 – Development of a plan for the procurement of Canadian Coast Guard vessels, and particularly icebreakers, required for adequate surveillance, monitoring, control of, and assistance to, surface and undersea craft operating in the CNWP;

8 – Development of a plan for the procurement of a fleet of naval vessels, particularly submarine craft and ice-capable surface vessels for

military surveillance and transportation duties in the CNWP especially relating to enforcement;

9 – Development of a plan for the provision of all the services that Canada should offer transiting ships for the safe and efficient operation of the CNWP;

10 – Development of a plan for converting the voluntary NORDREG vessel traffic management system, operating only part of the year, to a year-round, compulsory system;

11 – Development of a plan for an undersea system for the detection and monitoring of undersea craft entering the Canadian Arctic;

12 – Development of scenarios of various possible disasters that should be envisaged in the CNWP and the development of Disaster Mitigation Plans for adequately coping with them;

13 – Development of a schedule of potential yearly revenue that could be generated from user and service fees from a CNWP open to maritime traffic.

14 – Development of a plan to negotiate partnering with various interested parties for sharing the costs associated with creating and operating all the systems required for safe and adequate maritime operations in the Northwest Passage.

15 – Development of a budget for all the above spread over an appropriate number of years.[1]

* Canadian Northwest Passage

Notes

PART I: ROALD AMUNDSEN AND THE *GJØA*, 1903–06

1. "Journey Into China" in Danforth, Kenneth C. (ed.), *Journey into China* (Washington: National Geographic Society, 1982). 181
2. John Rae (1813–1893), a Scottish explorer from the Orkney Islands, confirmed the existence of a Northwest Passage by discovering the last unknown, 100 kilometre (60 mile) stretch of sea link from the Atlantic Ocean to the Pacific through the Arctic Islands.
3. All unattributed quotations in Part I are from Roald Amundsen, *The North West Passage* Vols. I and II (New York: E.P. Dutton, 1908).
4. Roald Amundsen, *My Life As An Explorer* (Garden City, NY: Doubleday, 1927). 28
5. Fridtjoff Nansen (1861–1932) is arguably Norway's greatest national hero—explorer, scientist, oceanographer, athlete, international statesman, humanitarian and Nobel Laureate for peace. He was the first to cross the Greenland icecap on skis. Tavelling with Otto Sverdrup on the famous *Fram,* he made a dash for the North Pole, reaching a point farthest north for the time, but not the pole.
6. The Deutsche Seewarte Institute (German Navel Observatory) of Hamburg, Germany was, and still is, a world-renowned institute for the study of science, mathematics and technology. Amundsen went to the Institute to consult Geheimrath George von Neumayer, at that time one of the world's pre-eminent experts on magnetism.
7. Otto Sverdrup, *New Land* Vol. I (London: Longmans, Green, and Co, 1904) 89. For more information on Captain Otto Sverdrup, see Gerard Kenney, *Ships of Wood and Men of Iron: A Norwegian-Canadian Saga of Exploration in the High Arctic* (Toronto: Natural Heritage, 2005).
8. Henry A. Larsen, (with Frank R. Sheer and Edward Olmholt-Jensen, *The Big Ship* (Toronto: McClelland & Stewart, 1967) 10.
9. Leonard Gutteridge, *Ghosts of Cape Sabine* (New York: G.P. Putnam's Sons, 2000) 54–55.
10. Ludvig Mylius Erichsen (1872–1907) was a Danish journalist and explorer who led two expeditions to Greenland: one to study the language and culture of the Polar Inuit during which he met Amundsen, and a second to

chart the northern coast of Greenland. Tragically, he perished on the second expedition.

11. Peter Freuchen (1886–1957) was a Dane who spent a good part of his in life in Greenland and came to live like an Inuit. He and Knud Rasmussen established a trading post at Thule. Freuchen travelled widely in Greenland. On one of his trips, overtaken by a blizzard, he lost a foot to frost. He was also a superb raconteur who molded facts a bit to fit a good story. Freuchen wrote several books on Inuit, his most known being *Book of the Eskimos,* published by World Fawcett World Library of New York in 1961 and edited by his wife, Dagmar Freuchen.

12. James Clark Ross (1800–1862) explored extensively in the polar regions at both ends of the earth. He is famous for being the discoverer the site of the wandering north magnetic pole on Boothia Peninsula in 1831 while on an expedition with his uncle John Ross. Amundsen was the second person to pin down the pole on his voyage through the Northwest Passage from 1903 to 1906 described in this book.

13. Albert Peter Low (1861–1942) was one of Canada's foremost geologists at a time when practising that profession required the hardened physique of a coureur de bois. He was surveying northern Québec and Labrador for the Canadian Geological Survey when OttO Sverdrup and his crew were discovering new land in Canada's Arctic Archipelago at the turn of the century. Low put a vast area of wilderness Canada on the map at the end of the 1800s. His explorations and surveying in the years from 1893 to 1895 laid the groundwork for the definition of the Québec-Labrador border. For more information on A.P. Low, see Gerard Kenney, *Ships of Wood and Men of Iron: A Norwegian-Canadian Saga of Exploration in the High Arctic* (Toronto: Natural Heritage Books, 2005) 93–103. See also Max Finkelstein and James Stone, *Paddling the Boreal Forest: Rediscovering A.P. Low* (Toronto: Natural Heritage Books, 2004).

14. Sir Allen William Young (1830–?) was born in Twickenham, Middlesex, England, in 1830. In 1875, he undertook a private expedition to navigate the Northwest Passage in a single season, and to try and find more information about Franklin's fate. However, ice barred his progress and the expedition failed.

15. Geological Survey of Canada Web site, 2005, http://gsc.nrcan.gc.ca/geomag/nmp/expeditions_e.php. *Geomagnetism—History of Expeditions to the North Magnetic Pole.* Ottawa, accessed on April 13, 2006.

16. Ibid.

17. There were two men named Hansen on the expedition: Lieutenant

Godfred Hansen and Seaman Helmer Hansen. To distinguish between them, Lieutenant Hansen will be referred to as Lt. Hansen and Seaman Hansen simply as Hansen.

18. Today's Inuit at Gjoa Haven say that there were three men. See David F.Pelly, "Commemorating Roald Amundsen's Northwest Passage" in *Above & Beyond*, November/December 2003, 34.

19. Ibid.

20. See Graham W. Rowley, *Cold Comfort* (Montreal/Kingston: McGill-Queen's University Press, 1996).

21. Radio program by Alex Chadwick in the NPR/National Geographic Exploration series, "The Geographic Century," March 8, 1999.

22. Robert Falcon Scott (1868–1912) was an English naval officer who led a famed, but ill-fated expedition to reach the South Pole in 1910–13. He and four companions did reach the pole, only to find out that Roald Amundsen had beat them to it by a month. Scott and his four companions perished on the return trip.

23. Henry A. Larsen (with Frank R. sheer and Edward Olmholt-Jansen), *The Big Ship* (Toronto: McClelland & Stewart Limited, 1967) 121.

PART II: HENRY ASBJORN LARSEN AND THE *ST. ROCH*, 1940–44

1. George Kish, *North-east Passage; Adolf Erik Nordenskiöld, His Life and Times* (Amsterdam: Nico Israel, 1973)

2. Henry A. Larsen (with Frank R. Sheer and Edvard Olmholt-Jansen), *The Big Ship: An Autobiography* (Toronto/Montreal: McClelland & Stewart, 1967) 10. All following unattributed quotations are from *The Big Ship*.

3. Christian "Charlie" Klengenberg (1869–1931) was a white whaler turned trader who sailed to a number of western Arctic communities bringing needed supplies to the Inuit in return for several of their products, mainly furs. Charlie married an Inuit woman and settled on Victoria Island where they raised a large family of boys and girls and taught them the best of two worlds, Inuit and white. The boys lived as Inuit and became as good at surviving, if not better, than they. Both boys and girls were home-schooled by their parents to a high degree of skills and knowledge needed to survive in the modern society of the time. Klengenberg and Larsen became fast friends and sailed together to many Arctic communities during which Larsen gained valuable skills in Arctic sailing.

4. Mitch Owens Drive in Ottawa is named in his honour.

5. Henry Larsen married Mary Hargreaves on February 7, 1935. Their first child, a daughter named Doreen, was born while he was on patrol. Likewise, both her brother Gordon and her sister Beverly were born

when Henry was away. He never knew any of his children before they were anywhere from one-and-a-half to two years old.

PART III: CANADIAN SOVEREIGNTY AND THE ENVIRONMENT IN THE NORTHWEST PASSAGE ARE AT RISK

1. Stan Rogers, "Northwest Passage," ©1981. Used by permission of Fogarty's Cove Music.
2. Susan Joy Hassol, *Impacts of a Warming Arctic: Arctic Climate Impact Assessment* (Cambridge, UK; New York, NY: Cambridge University Press, 2004). The book is on a CD-ROM put out by Cambridge University, see page 14.
3. A nautical mile, or knot, is approximately equivalent to 1.853 kilometres of 1.152 statute miles.
4. The article is in UNCLOS, the United Nations Convention on the Law of the Sea, which is available on the UN web site.
5. *Canadian Yearbook of International Law*, No. 12 (1974) (Vancouver: University of British Columbia) 279.
6. "Canada proceedings of Standing Committee on External Affairs and National Defence," Vol. 24 (May 22, 1975) 6.
7. Erik Brüel, *International Straits: A Treatise on International Law*, Vol. 1 (London: Sweet and Maxwell) 42, 43.
8. The complete text of Joe Clark's statement is included in Appendix I. It is recommended reading for those who wish to appreciate its full value.
9. "Position Statement at the Beaufort Sea Environment Assessment Panel," Appendix I (Canadian Department of Transport, 1982) 22–3.
10. The present Arctic class system of designating the ice-capability of ships is currently evolving into a new system in which the existing Arctic class numbers are replaced by Canadian Arctic Category or CAC numbers. There is no direct equivalency between the existing Arctic Classes and the new Canadian Arctic Categories.

APPENDIX II

1. If deemed appropriate, items 6 and 8 could be combined with the broader Department of National Defence requirements for similar services.

Bibliography

Amundsen, Roald, *The North West Passage* Vols. I and II. (New York: E.P. Dutton, 1908).

_____, *My Life As An Explorer* (Garden City, NY: Doubleday, 1927).

Bassett, John, *Henry Larsen* (Don Mills, ON: Fitzhenry and Whiteside, 1980).

Beattie, Owen and John Geiger, *Frozen in Time* (Saskatoon, SK: Western Producer Prairie Books, 1987).

Berg, Kåre, *Heroes of the Polar Wastes* (Norway: Andresen & Butenschfn Forlag, 2003).

Bernier, J.E. (Translated by Paul Therrien), *Les Mémoires de J.E. Bernier* (Montreal: Les Quinze, 1983).

Bernier, J.E., *Cruise of the Arctic 1906–07* (Ottawa: Government Printing Bureau, 1907).

_____, *Cruise of the Arctic 1908–09* (Ottawa: Government Printing Bureau, 1909).

_____, *Cruise of the Arctic 1910–11* (Ottawa: Government Printing Bureau, 1911).

Bruel, Eric, *International Straits*, Vol. 1 (London: Sweet and Maxwell, 1947))

Delgado, James P, *Across the Top of the World: The Quest for the Northwest Passage.* (Vancouver: Douglas & McIntyre, 1999).

_____, *Dauntless St. Roch: The Mounties' Arctic Schooner* (Victoria, BC: Horsdal and Schubart Publishers, 1992).

_____, *Arctic Workhorse: The RCMP Schooner St. Roch* (Victoria BC: Touchwood Editions, 2003).

Dennett, John Frederick, *The Voyages and Travels of Captains Ross, Parry, Franklin and Mr. Belzoni* (London: William Wright, 1835).

Dorion-Robitaille, Yolande, *Captain J.E. Bernier's Contributions to Canadian Sovereignty in the Arctic* (Ottawa: Ministry of Indian and Northern Affairs, Canada, 1978).

Fairley, T.C. and Charles E. Israel, *The True North* (London: MacMillan, 1957).

Griffiths, Franklyn (ed.), *Politics of the Northwest Passage* (Montreal/Kingston: McGill-Queen's University Press, 1967).

Guttridge, Leonard F., *Ghosts of Cape Sabine* (New York: G.P. Putnam's Sons, 2000).

Huntford, Roland (ed.), *The Amundsen Photographs* (New York: Atlantic Monthly Press, 1987).

Imbert, Bertrand, *North Pole South Pole: Journey to the Ends of the Earth* (New York: H.N. Abrams, 1992).

Keating, Bern, *The Northwest Passage* (New York/Chicago/San Francisco: Rand McNally & Company, 1970).

Kenney, Gerard, *Arctic Smoke & Mirrors* (Prescott, ON: Voyageur Publishing, 1994).

_____, *Ships of Wood and Men of Iron* (Regina, SK: Canadian Plains Research Centre, University of Regina, 2004. Reprint by Natural Heritage Books of Toronto, 2005).

Kish, George, *North-east passage; Adolf Erik Nordenskiöld: His Life and Times* (Amsterdam: Nico Israel, 1973).

Lamson, Cynthia and David L. Vanderzwagg (eds), *Transit Management in the Northwest Passage* (Cambridge, UK: Cambridge University Press, 1988).

Larsen, Henry A, "Our Return Voyage Through the North-west Passage," *RCMP Quarterly*, April 1945).

_____, (with Frank R. Sheer and Edvard Olmholt-Jansen), *The Big Ship*, (Toronto: McClelland & Stewart Limited, 1967).

_____, *The North West Passage* (Ottawa: The Queen's Printer, 1969).

Loomis, Chauncey C., *Weird and Tragic Shores* (New York: Alfred A. Knopf. 1971).

Low, A.P., *The Cruise of the Neptune* (Ottawa: Government Printing Bureau, 1906).

MacDonald, R.St.J. (ed.), *The Arctic Frontier* (Toronto: University of Toronto Press, 1966).

Minotto, Claude, *La Frontière Arctique du Canada: Les expéditions de Joseph-Elzéar Bernier, Master's thesis, McGill University, Montreal, 1975*.

Nansen, Fridtjof, *Farthest North* Vols, I and II (London: MacMillan and Co. Ltd., 1897).

Osborne, Season, *Closing the Front Door of the Arctic,* Master's thesis, (Ottawa: Carleton University, Ottawa, 2003.

Pharand, Donat, *Canada's Arctic Waters in International Law* (Cambridge UK: Cambridge University Press, 1988).

_____, *International Straits of the World, the Northwest Passage: Arctic Straits* (Boston/Lancaster/Dordrecht: Martinus Nijhoff Publishers, 1984).

Rasmussen, Knud, *Across Arctic America: Narrative of the Fifth Thule Expedition* (New York: Greenwood Press, 1969

_____, "East Through the North-West Passage," *RCMP Quarterly*, Ottawa, October 1942.

RCMP, *Reports and Other Papers relating to the voyages of the RCM Police Schooner "St. Roch" Through the North West Passage* (Ottawa: The King's Printer, 1945).

Robinson, J. Lewis, "Conquest of the Northwest Passage by RCMP Schooner St. Roch," *Canadian Geographical Journal,* Vol. 30, No. 2, Ottawa, 1945.

Ross, M.J., *Polar Pioneers John Ross and James Clark Ross* (Montreal/Kingston: McGill-Queen's University Press, 1994).

Rowley, Graham W., *Cold Comfort* (Montreal/Kingston: McGill-Queen's University Press, 1996).

Savoury, Ann, *The Search for the North West Passage* (New York: St. Martins Press, 1999).

Struzik, Edward, *The Quest for an Arctic Route to the East* (Toronto: Key Porter Books, 1991).

Sverdrup, Otto, *New Land* Vols. I and II (London: Longmans, Green and Co, 1904).

Thompson, John B., *The More Northerly Route* (Ottawa: Indian and Northern Affairs – Park Canada, 1974).

Tranter, G.J., *Plowing the Arctic* (Toronto: Longman's Green & Company, 1945).

Wilkinson, Doug, *Arctic Fever* (Toronto: Clarke, Irwin & Company Limited, 1971).

Williams, Glyn, *Voyages of Delusion* (New Haven: Yale University Press, 2002).

Zaslow, Morris (ed.), *A Century of Canada's Arctic Islands* (Ottawa: Royal Society of Canada, 1981).

Index

About the Author

Gerard Kenney (his friends call him Gerry) was born in St. Rémi d'Amherst not far from Mont-Tremblant, Québec, in 1931. Though a Canadian, he spent the first sixteen years of his life in New York City except for the months of July and August, which he enjoyed in the small French-Canadian village of his birth. In 1948, he returned to his native Canada and has lived there ever since.

Gerry's work as a telecommunications engineer has taken him to many countries of the world as well as to the northern reaches of his native land. Working for Bell Canada in the '60s and '70s, Gerry was responsible for the engineering aspects of the telephone system based on short-wave radio that served the eastern half of the Northwest Territories, Labrador and Nouveau Québec.

In the late '60s, while he was travelling on Ellesmere Island, an RCMP officer in Grise Fiord showed him the horizontal member of a wooden burial cross which had been found nearby. It was in memory of a Norwegian sailor, Ove Braskerud, who had left his bones in the frigid waters of nearby Harbour Fiord in 1899. Braskerud had been a member of the 1898–1902 Sverdrup expedition aboard the Norwegian ship *Fram* that discovered and explored high Arctic islands lying north of the Canadian mainland. That chance encounter with Braskerud's cross is what led Gerry to write books about the Arctic.